INTERNATIONAL FOOTBALL BOOK

No. 18

Leighton James of Derby County whose transfer from Burnley cost £300,000. With money in short supply and top quality players even more difficult to find, it could be some time before another British player moves for such a fee.

INTERNATIONAL FOOTBALL BOOK

No. 18

Edited by Eric Batty

with contributions by

TERRY YORATH   PHIL THOMPSON   SAMMY McILROY

WIM VAN HANEGEM   TONY TOWERS   ROBERTO MARTINEZ

KENNY DALGLISH   DON GIVENS   MIKE DOYLE

SEPP MAIER   TREVOR BROOKING   MILJAN MILJANIC

RAY GRAYDON   RUUD GEELS   STEWART BARROWCLOUGH

BRIAN GLANVILLE

SOUVENIR PRESS LTD LONDON

ISBN 0 285 62230 7

Filmset by BAS Printers Limited, Wallop, Hampshire and printed in Great Britain by Morrison and Gibb Ltd

CONTENTS

LIST OF ILLUSTRATIONS

Photographs provided by

Sporting Pictures (UK) Ltd.,
7a, Lambs Conduit Passage,
Holborn, London WC1.

MANCHESTER UNITED'S SECRET IS TOMMY DOCHERTY'S FAITH IN HIS PLAYERS

says . . . . SAMMY McILROY

Manchester United and Northern Ireland star

Sammy McIlroy flicks the ball towards goal against Oxford in Manchester United's successful bid to bounce back into Division One, first time.

FOR a young reserve with a big club like Manchester United, breaking into the first team is not at all an easy thing to do. But in my case, as with many others who join the club straight from school and have to live away from home, the early years can present even bigger problems. Different, but bigger.

Just imagine it. You are playing in schoolboy football in Belfast when Bob Bishop, Manchester United's scout in Northern Ireland asks if you'd be interested. Of course you would, and then after someone from Manchester has come over to see you play it's all arranged and you sign as an apprentice for United.

Then the problems start for as I found, although the club couldn't have done more to help me whatever they did, there is no way to overcome feeling scared and lonely as I was. Coming from Belfast and the security of a home background, Manchester is a very big place—and seems twice as big as it is.

Like many other football apprentices I lived in lodgings and I can't thank my landladies enough for all their help and kindness. But though the club helped by arranging for me to go home once a month even during the season, each time I had a few days at home I didn't want to go back to Manchester.

It's all different now, happily married and settled in Manchester I feel at home there and would never dream of leaving United. But looking back, the first two years or so were the most critical in my career.

My time as a United player has coincided with one of their most difficult periods with players like Bobby Charlton and Denis Law passing their peak and George Best quitting the club. There's no way you can replace such players overnight—if ever.

As everyone knows we were relegated but what happened to United should serve as a warning to other clubs that fail to bring in good young players in time. In my opinion, if Manchester United can be relegated then any other club can go the same way.

It was Frank O'Farrell who gave me my first opportunity in the senior team and I had the good fortune to score the first goal on my debut in a 3–3 draw with Manchester City. I shall always be grateful to him for giving me my big chance but

Manchester United's relegation should serve as a warning that none of the top clubs are safe . . . says McIlroy. The departure of players like Denis Law (above) and Bobby Charlton, allied to George Best (in action, right) proved too great a loss and underlines the fact that even the greatest clubs must develop young replacements and blood them in good time if a crisis is to be avoided.

the only manager I've really known at United has been Tommy Docherty.

Though we have known success and failure, Tommy Docherty never ceases to exude confidence. He bubbles with it and it's infectious, spreading naturally to the players. He's the kind of man that will fight all the way for his players and he has the knack of inspiring everyone around him. After listening to his pre-match team talk, you really feel good and at half time, no matter what the score he never loses confidence. 'I have faith in you' he says 'you can bounce back' . . . and you'd be surprised how many times he's been proved right.

We were desperately unlucky to be relegated anyhow. We finished up at the end of that season playing really well and everyone bar Tommy Docherty was down in the dumps when it was finally settled. He may have felt it, but he never let it show and the most important thing was that we retained our team spirit, the club didn't die.

That was, I think, what made it possible for us to win the Second Division championship after only one season. We didn't expect to stay in the lower league for long but it was a wonderful feeling when we'd clinched promotion and after that there was never any doubt about us going up as champions.

We would never have been relegated had we signed Stuart Pearson (in action above) earlier, says McIlroy. Pearson has added more than punch and pace to the United attack and together with their two wingers Steve Coppell (right) and Gordon Hill (left) has done much to re-instate Manchester United as a powerful advocate of attacking football. Amongst the first clubs to bring back real wingers, United's lead deserves to be rewarded and it is hoped will be widely copied.

Everyone believed in themselves and each other too much to let that honour slip away.

Perhaps the key man for us was Stuart Pearson who joined us from Hull just before our relegation was settled. If we'd had him earlier—a really outstanding spearhead goalgetter and target-man, then I'm sure we would not have gone down.

We proved that last season I think, getting off to a great start in Division I, always within a point or two of the leaders and on top ourselves for several periods. The secrets of our success (if there are any secrets) were Mr. Docherty's unshakeable faith in his players and the fact that as a squad we had been together for about three years.

Manchester United must have the greatest lot of supporters in the world. At home you can almost guarantee a 50,000 crowd every time we play and away from home we invariably break ground records for attendances. It's tragic that there's a small hooligan element amongst them but I think the stories are blown up by the newspapers simply because it involves Manchester United.

Internationally I earned my first cap in a 1–1 draw against Spain in the days when Terry Neill now manager of Spurs was in charge of Northern Ireland. Since then I think I've earned myself a regular place in the side and though I don't want to seem conceited I'd be disappointed if I was left out—and I'll be disappointed too if we don't make some kind of impact in the 1978 World Cup qualifying matches.

We were really unlucky in the European Championship, beating Yugoslavia 1–0 in our first game and then seeing the Yugoslavs qualify for the quarter finals. The vital game was away to Norway in Oslo and after leading 1–0, we lost 2–1 and that was a ridiculous result that had nothing to do with the way the game went. After that it was all uphill.

Although it was a bit rough to see Yugoslavia qualify from our group in the European championship after we'd beaten them in Belfast I have nothing but admiration for Yugoslav football. Their inside forward Branko Oblak is quite brilliant with Ivan Buljan not far behind him for skill.

Before the start of last season 1975–76, the depth of the Yugoslav's talent was really impressed on me when we met one of their top clubs, Red Star of Belgrade. This was a pre-season friendly match at

Old Trafford and we drew 4–4 with them after a truly remarkable game. Red Star were really terrific, one of the best sides I have ever seen or played against. On the night I thought every one of their ten outfield players was World class.

Red Star's performance brings out something I have always believed. You must have a really high degree of confidence to be really good and I find it frustrating when I hear the moaners and see what the critics write in print, every time a British team is beaten.

I am convinced there are too many people knocking the game instead of trying to build it up. At international level I'd like to see our top players get a lot more praise and support—encourage them and cheer them on, and I'm sure that you'll find that the players will respond.

Sammy McIlroy in action (right) and below, Petar Krivokuca, the Red Star international right back with more than 40 caps and more skill than many forwards, who so impressed against Manchester United.

'THE OLD LIVERPOOL FIGHT IS STILL THERE...'

By

PHIL THOMPSON

of Liverpool F.C.

Phil Thompson in action (left) and as number 4 (below) the meat in a Spurs sandwich.

17

ALTHOUGH I played for the England Youth team in 1972 and got an Under 23 cap later my biggest thrill in football so far was to help Liverpool win the FA Cup when we beat Newcastle 3–0 at Wembley. I'd been there before but never actually played on the hallowed turf. My previous visit was as a Liverpool supporter—I'd been a pro with them for about 4 months when they were beaten 2–1 in the final by Arsenal—and that winning goal scored by Charlie George really sickened me.

Though I was already a Liverpool player I'd been one of their biggest supporters all my life. With a family like mine, Liverpool born and with 2 brothers, 4 sisters and a mother and father all Liverpool mad, you can't be anything but a Liverpool fan.

My family is also the reason why I am not bothered whether the Professional Footballers Association win their battle for freedom of contract for in my situation, quite apart from what I owe the club, my family would never let me leave no matter how much money I was offered elsewhere.

The resignation of Bill Shankly (above) gave Phil Thompson the biggest shock of his career, while Charlie George (pictured right, in action for Derby County) sickened him when he scored the winning goal in the FA Cup Final for Arsenal against Liverpool. On a happier note, Thompson struck up an immediate understanding with Emlyn Hughes (left) and together they form the twin pillars of the Liverpool defence.

19

Another big day that sticks in my memory was in 1973 when with two games to play we were at home to Leeds and had to win to take the championship. We were at home and Anfield was packed and with about ten thousand fans locked out I almost missed the kick off because it was so difficult to get through the crowds to the dressing room. I was only 19 at the time with about a dozen first team games behind me and we beat Leeds 2–0. You can imagine how I felt, sitting in the bath after that one.

But the biggest shock was the day I heard the news that Bill Shankly had resigned. I couldn't believe it. I remember someone telling me they'd heard about it on the radio and I said he was a liar. It seemed impossible. Bill Shankly was Liverpool!

There's no doubt about it, Shanks was unique and there'll never be another one quite like him. Apart from what he did for Liverpool, he did so much for the game as a whole.

Bob Paisley stepped up to take charge of the team, but in the dressing room it seemed unreal at first. Fortunately, once we got out on the park everyone got on with the job of playing for the club and it's never been anything but the same old Liverpool. It just seemed different without having Shanks there.

The most effective striking force in English soccer is undoubtedly the Liverpool duo, Kevin Keegan (pictured in action, facing page) and big John Toshack (above) who play so well together they seem to read each others mind. Near left is Bob Paisley who took over as manager after Bill Shankly's departure with such good effect that the entire Liverpool squad soon wanted 'to win something, just for Bob'.

Bob Paisley proved how good a manager he was, firstly by never attempting to become another Bill Shankly. Now he's proved he's a great boss in his own right. His first thoughts are for his players. If the players are all right then he's all right, and very soon all the lads wanted to win something for Bob.

In the old days Shanks used to go around the dressing room telling everyone how great they were, building up their confidence and belief in themselves, in each other and in Liverpool. Bob Paisley was there too and his role was to be a counter to Shanks and keep everyone's feet on the ground.

Nothing has changed really under Bob Paisley. We still train the same way to the same time-tables laid down in Shanks' time and with the same training and coaching staff.

I owe a great deal to all the backroom boys at Anfield. Liverpool born, I was an apprentice with the club, playing in those days in midfield but always being better at the defensive side of the game. I was still a midfield player in the reserves though I had played in the back four a couple of times when the club were in difficulties through injuries. It was Bill Shankly who gave me the central stopper role when Larry Lloyd was injured one day. He had played me at right back in a Cup game with Doncaster and I must have done quite well and from there he got the idea of switching me.

With Larry unfit, Bill put me in to play with Emlyn Hughes at the back and we seemed to hit off an immediate understanding. Anyway we played about ten games together in the middle without conceding a single goal.

But if it was Bill Shankly that gave me the chance to become a first team player there are other unsung, possibly unknown men at Anfield to whom I owe so much. Ruben Bennett, the first team trainer was a great morale booster when you needed lifting up. And Joe Fagan who ran the reserve team when I was in it, was in much the same mould. But he could hand out a roasting too when needed. I remember after my first game for the Reserves, Joe took me aside and said 'look son, you've been in the game long enough. You have got to get your game together. Almost every ball you played today was back towards your own goal.'

Then there was Ronnie Moran who steered me through the Liverpool Youth teams. After I had

A comparative newcomer to the Liverpool side Phil Neal (pictured above). Outside Liverpool's Keegan and Toshack, Phil Thompson reckons the Ipswich Town strikers David Johnson and Trevor Whymark are one of the best scoring pairs in the country, particularly after they starred in Ipswich stealing a point from Anfield early in 1976 where they drew 3–3. Johnson (seen in a tussle, above right) with Frankie Gray and Gordon McQueen of Leeds, 'has improved tremendously since leaving Everton', says Thompson, who also feels that Whymark (below right in a duel with Norman Hunter) is specially dangerous in the air.

played for the England Youth XI I got a bit big-headed and he warned me that if I didn't get my feet back on the ground, I'd get nowhere.

Ronnie had more to do with my success than anyone. I remember sitting next to him after we'd beaten Leicester in the FA Cup semi-final at Villa Park and trying to thank him. With my ticket to Wembley I said to him 'Thanks for everything. It's because of you that I am where I am now.' Ronnie wouldn't have it. 'I only did my job' he said, 'if you didn't have it in you I could have done nothing with you.' But I know deep down that I owe him more than I can ever repay.

As for our good run last season I really believe that although football is a team game, much of our success was due to Kevin Keegan and John Toshack. Kevin had a really good season, playing up front in home games but adapting his game to play in midfield away from home and breaking forward from there.

On last seasons form John Toshack must be the best front man in the country and he played so well with Kevin. They play superbly together, feeding off each other, they seem to be able to read each others mind.

With Keegan and Toshack playing so well and Emlyn Hughes still at his best despite losing his England place we are going to remain high on the list of challengers for the top honours for some time.

Last season we got off to a bad start, losing 2–0 away to Q.P.R., and then in our first home game being held to a 2–2 draw by West Ham. Then we were 2–0 down to Spurs but the old Liverpool fight was still there and we came back to win 3–2. Everyone gets off to a bad start now and again but we shook that off at a time when the critics were saying Liverpool were over the top and beat Leeds 3–0.

After that we never looked back though we had a bit of a shock when Ipswich came to Anfield and drew 3–3 early in the New Year. We don't like giving points away at Anfield but in my opinion David Johnson and Trevor Whymark are two of the best strikers in the country. Whymark is specially dangerous in the air and Johnson has improved beyond recognition since he left Everton.

Whymark and Johnson are dangerous all right, but I'm sure everyone connected with Liverpool will agree there's no attacking pair to equal our duo, Keegan and Toshack.

Kevin Keegan (dark shorts) slips a tackle by Bryan Hamilton of Ipswich Town.

OLEG BLOKHIN

RUSSIA'S LEFT WING STAR WHO WAS VOTED THE BEST PLAYER IN EUROPE FOR 1975

— ★ —

FOR several years past, the image of soccer in the U.S.S.R., has been one of dull defensive play and Scandinavian-type, thick-legged players lacking both elasticity and ingenuity and playing like robots. But in 1975, Dynamo Kiev burst onto the international scene, taking the European Cup Winners Cup to Russia, the first major club tournament the Soviets have won and spearheading the Dynamo attack was left winger Oleg Blokhin, a most un-Russian type player of real quality.

Though it may not be widely appreciated abroad, the Soviet Union is a very big country, bigger than the whole of Western Europe and to assume that a Russian is a Russian is to make a very great mistake. The people from Moscow, Siberia and the Ukraine differ from each other in almost as many ways as do the Italians, the Dutch and the English. And in the Ukraine, where Blokhin was born in Kiev on October 5th, 1952, the people are more like Hungarians or Yugoslavs, exuberant, gay and outward looking. Certainly quite different from the stolid, dour image of the Russian people that is prevalent in Western Europe.

Oleg Blokhin (photo right) has been Russia's Footballer of the Year for the last three years and their top goalscorer in four consecutive seasons since 1972.

This exuberance and almost Latin temperament shows in the football of Dynamo Kiev whose players are both individualistic and artistic. Vladimir Muntjan and Anatolij Bychewecz, both from Dynamo Kiev stood out in the Russian 1970 World Cup team as untypical Russians. Oleg Blokhin goes even further; quick, lithe, supple, supremely gifted in his control of the ball and a regular goalscorer.

Blokhin first appeared on the international scene in the 1972 Olympic Games soccer tournament but dominated by track and field, the soccer gets little publicity and barely any television coverage except in the countries taking part. Thus, though Blokhin, only 19, scored 6 goals (a total second only to Poland's Kazimierz Deyna) and helped Russia to third place, the event passed almost unnoticed.

Oleg Blokhin (portrait below) and right, in white, in action in a Russian league match against Zarja Vorochilovgrad.

In the Russian 1972 season (spring to autumn) Blokhin was the top scorer with 14 goals and though he has now become a very well marked man wherever he plays, he has retained this title for four consecutive seasons. In 1973 he raised his total to 18; in 1974 to 20 and last season, the 1975 campaign, he was again the top marksman with 18.

Blokhin was born into a sporting background, his father was a footballer while his mother Ekaterina Adamenko was at one time the 440 metres hurdles champion of the Ukraine. His father wanted him to play football, but his mother, fearful that he might be injured, perhaps seriously, urged him to take up athletics. He did both, clocking 10·8 seconds for 100 metres at his best and joined the Dynamo Kiev football section as a boy. When not studying or training he spent much of his time just kicking a ball around.

This familiarity with the ball shows itself in his electrifying bursts on the left wing. Predominantly left footed, he is not particularly good in the air and his right foot is almost a 'swinger', but with the ball at his feet he is composed, quick off the mark and tantalising in his dribbles.

Blokhin admits that in his teens, his idol was the Yugoslav left wing star Dragan Dzajic who he

Photo left depicts Anatolij Bychewecz, Blokhin's predecessor as left-wing-cum-centre-forward for the U.S.S.R. and Dynamo Kiev, a star in the 1970 World Cup. Above, Leonid Burjak, Blokhin's inside-left partner whose skills and intelligence provide passes that enable him to use his pace and shooting power.

admired for his skill with the ball and his calm, deliberate scoring ability with crafty flicks and deadly 'chips'.

Since the 1974 World Cup which he followed closely on television, Blokhin has now become an admirer of Johan Cruyff and in his play he displays a little bit of both.

With the ball positioned inside his delicate left foot, Blokhin has the balance of Dzajic, the skill to

Photo above shows Blokhin with the ball slipping past Giacinto Facchetti (dark shirt on the left), who has more than 80 caps, in the Russia–Italy game in 1975 which Russia won, 1–0.

Dragan Dzajic (above) the Yugoslav international left-winger who was the idol of Blokhin's teens and the player on whom he tried to model himself.

machine, he used to delight in long mazy runs that took him past man after man.

Elected Russia's Footballer of the Year in 1973, he retained this title a year later and when interviewed early in 1975 (when he took the trophy for the third consecutive season) he made a string of shrewd observations. Asked about his style of play he confessed that he had been bullied by his coaches and manager to be less of an individual and had consciously tried to adapt his game, to use his skills for the benefit of the team. His coaches had wanted him to turn the defence when he was forced away from goal, sprinting to the goal-line to pull the ball back for a colleague to shoot. But until he saw the 1974 World Cup and noted the play of Cruyff, Beckenbauer and the Polish left winger Robert Gadocha he hadn't been very successful in this. 'Then' he said 'it suddenly clicked in my mind, seeing it done, and I am sure I learned a lot about aspects of the game that were new to me.' 'Cruyff' he went on 'is a great individual but plays within the team framework rather than on his own. I realise now that even the greatest player is useless without the help of his colleagues.'

Blokhin was not alone in being impressed by the football of Holland in the World Cup. The Kiev club officials and all Blokhin's colleagues are now eager to match the class and style of Holland, to play what has been termed 'total football' and give it a Ukrainian twist.

Asked what qualities a goalscorer needed, Blokhin answered with a bluntness that is rare amongst scorers today . . . 'the basic factor is to get rid of fear. Fear of being hurt must be banished from your mind and you must go blindly into the best attacking positions.'

Wiser than he was at 20, Blokhin can understand now why his coaches tried to bully him as he described it, into being more unselfish. He is trying to balance his game between scoring goals himself and creating chances for others.

Blokhin confessed to having mixed feelings about 1974 . . . 'we won the Cup and League in Russia and I was the leading scorer but for the national team I played very badly when we lost 3–0 to the Republic of Ireland in Dublin. That came at the end of our season and spoiled the year for me' he said.

get by his opponent and the speed off the mark of Cruyff. More than that, his 100 metre pace makes him faster than Dzajic or Cruyff over 30 to 40 yards and before he settled down to play a more mature game, becoming a part in Dynamo's well oiled

But 1975 more than atoned for that failure in Dublin. Walking away from all their rivals in the championship, Dynamo retained their title in the league and Blokhin was again top scorer. With Dynamo Kiev representing the U.S.S.R. at international level, results improved and in Basle they beat Ferencvaros of Hungary 3–0 in the final of the European Cupwinners Cup.

They followed that with a tremendous triumph in the unofficial 'Supercup', the clash with the European Cup holders Bayern München. In Munich, Dynamo won by a single goal to nil and in Kiev they triumphed 2–0 . . . and all three goals were scored by Blokhin.

These three matches put Dynamo Kiev (and Blokhin) right in the forefront of the European press and at the end of 1975, Oleg was voted 'European Footballer of the Year', the second Russian to take this trophy, previously earned by the Dynamo Moscow goalkeeper Lev Yachin.

Igor Chislenko, in action above for Dynamo Moscow, the first Russian winger since 1945 to make an impact at international level. Chislenko was at his peak in the 1966 World Cup.

Unless serious injury intervenes, Blokhin seems destined to become one of world football's leading figures but he is the first to admit now that he owes a great deal to his Kiev colleagues. In particular the midfield players Vladimir Muntjan, Victor Kolotov and his young inside partner Leonid Burjak who work hard with skill and determination to win the ball and give him a stream of good passes.

Blokhin also pays tribute to his striking colleague Vladimir Onitchenko who like Oleg is naturally an outside left. Onitchenko switched to centre forward where his running off the ball pulls covering defenders out of Blokhin's path when he sets off on one of his dynamic thrusts towards goal. He has built up a real understanding with Onitchenko, always quick to position themselves to help each other, adept at giving and taking one-two's and making many goal chances for each other.

It says much for Onitchenko and his colleagues that they work so selflessly, content to play for the team and let Blokhin bask in the European sun, but as his club manager Valerij Lobanovski said after hearing of Blokhin's European award, he must keep his feet on the ground and not let all the publicity go to his head.

If he does, then Oleg Blokhin seems certain to become one of the outstanding players of the seventies, for he will not be 24 until October, 1976.

Lev Yachin in action below during his career with Dynamo Moscow, the club he now manages. In his playing days Yachin was rated by many experts to be the number one goalkeeper of his time and in 1963 he was voted 'European Footballer of the Year', the first Soviet player to gain this coveted award now equalled by Oleg Blokhin.

WALES ARE NO LONGER

Says TERRY YORATH
and
THE WELS

'Under manager Mike Smith there's a new feeling and it's no surprise to me that Wales have been successful in Europe'.

SOME people have come to believe that many players are not too interested in playing for their country, but at least as far as I'm concerned, nothing could be further from the truth. I always give 100% whatever shirt I'm wearing, and in fact, I am if anything, a little more keyed up when I play for Wales.

Playing for Leeds I am more relaxed; feeling perfectly at home, one of the boys. But with Wales I am the captain now and as we only get together a few times each season, I seem to have a deeper sense of responsibility.

Terry Yorath, portrait (right) and in action for Wales (on left), says that contrary to public opinion, he is more keyed up when playing for his country than he is for his club, but that doesn't mean that he ever gives less than a hundred per cent for Leeds United.

HE POOR RELATIONS

f LEEDS UNITED

APTAIN

Being the only country from the five teams in the British Isles to qualify in the European Championship last season was really tremendous but I honestly think Wales earned it. Everyone connected with the team has put a lot into it and we reaped the reward.

Under our new manager Mike Smith there's a new feeling. He was probably surprised to be given the job but he grabbed it with both hands. He really looks after the players, making them feel important and he's always ready to listen.

Previously the Welsh team had always been the poor relations. Dave Bowen our manager was only

Pictured above are some of the Welsh squad training together last season and on the facing page, a pictorial tribute to Arfon Griffiths, out of the big time for so long at club level but apparently able to reach the heights whenever he pulls on a Welsh shirt. Above right, Griffiths is beaten to the ball by Fritz Koncilia in Wales' 1–0 home win v Austria, but (below right) he is caught in the act of scoring the only goal of the game.

a part-time boss and with a club to manage couldn't possibly do all the things Mike has done.

We really did feel a poor lot before Mike Smith came. It may seem only a little thing but in the old days when I first played for Wales we had to carry our own playing gear and bring our own boots. Now we have the best strip money can buy, our boots are provided for us and the gear for all our games is in the care of an official. All we have to carry is our personal belongings.

Another little thing that has helped the Welsh outfit to feel more important was the appointment of Cyril Lea from Ipswich as our trainer. His predecessor came from little Wrexham though the man did his best at all times, but now we have a trainer from a First Division club. All the little things add up to make the players feel they are as good as England or Scotland.

But of course one has to admit readily that Mike Smith has more time and more control than Dave Bowen ever had.

I still remember quite vividly my first cap when I was only a reserve with Leeds. It was against Italy, Wales' last game in a World Cup qualifying group. I had a rough time, playing before a capacity

Mike Smith (pictured above) the Englishman who as Wales' first full-time team manager led them to success.

Wales might have had success earlier says Terry Yorath—in the 1974 World Cup in which they drew 1–1 with England at Wembley. John Toshack (photo below, left) puts Wales ahead early in that match, beating Bobby Moore and Ray Clemence, but (photo above) Norman Hunter saved England from defeat with one of his rare goals—from long range.

crowd at the Olympic Stadium in Rome was a really big game for me then and I was marking Luigi Riva who scored a hat trick for Italy in a 4–1 win!

Some people have explained Wales' success as the result of not having many players to choose from and therefore being forced to keep the same team together. Of course it must help if the same players stay together over a period but there's more to it than that. For example, though we have only a handful of players to choose from compared to England we did very well in our final qualifying game against Austria. Big John Toshack was out, our three first choice goalkeepers were all unfit and John Roberts couldn't play either.

If it helps to keep the same players together it can also lead to a lot of trouble when three star players are unfit.

I think we might have had success even earlier for at one stage I was convinced we could qualify in the 1974 World Cup. For one thing we drew 1–1 against England at Wembley, one up until Norman Hunter scored a long range goal—and Norman usually only gets one goal a season and he had to save that one for us.

We had already beaten Poland at home, and away in Chorzow I felt we only lost through inexperience. Before that match only three of our side had played at top level on the continent. After twenty minutes Wyn Davies opened the scoring with a header but the referee disallowed it and that was a let down for many of the lads. The atmosphere was electric and the game turned into a kicking match and Trevor Hockey was sent off. In the end we lost but I'm not so sure that our present, more experienced team would have lost that night.

For the next World Cup we've got what looks like a tough group being coupled with Scotland and Czechoslovakia. I know we can beat Scotland in Wales and I really don't think the Czechs are a better side than us. Certainly they will be difficult to beat in Prague or Bratislava but the way I see it, all three teams should win their home games and it looks likely to be settled on goals difference unless someone playing at home has a particularly disastrous night.

Not all the continental teams are unbeatable away from home. Finland who we beat 3–0 at Swansea and drew 1–1 away with, were a poor lot, as were Luxembourg.

The biggest disappointment to me however has been the Hungarians. Against Wales in Cardiff they were very good individually but a very bad side. It was the same with their champions Ujpest when I played against them for Leeds. They were all very skilful individually but their technique was very bad. Not one of their players was a good header of the ball and I haven't seen a Hungarian goalkeeper who can take the ball in the air. In my opinion the Hungarians are living on their past reputation.

For Wales the first choice XI are all key men. I'm sure Leighton James is the best winger in Britain and big John Toshack is now playing better than at any time. But one must not forget to mention Arfon Griffiths. Remembering how long he's been out of the big time he's done a really great job.

With Leeds we had got over our unsettled period quite early on last season and forgotten our disappointment of the European Cup Final. About the game in Paris we'd been told exactly how Bayern would play and if we had played that way too it could have ended up like a game of chess, going on for days. Neither team did themselves justice that night.

We should have had a penalty early on for a foul by Beckenbauer on Allan Clarke and the disallowing of Peter Lorimer's 'goal' must have been a hair-line decision. But in the end we got frustrated and started hitting up too many balls for Joe

Jordan's head. We knew what to expect from Bayern and got it. We knew what we had to do to beat them but in our frustration we lost our way.

Things haven't changed much at Leeds for we still have what is probably the best squad of players in Britain. Jimmy Armfield is now settled in and I have a great deal of respect for him. He's much more relaxed than Don Revie used to be, so much so that at times you get the feeling he isn't taking the game as seriously, but of course he is.

Appointing Don Howe to be our coach was a very good move—and a brave one I think. Don Howe is very widely respected as a coach for his knowledge of the game and a lesser man than Jimmy might have been afraid to appoint him.

I am enjoying my football more than ever nowadays. For one thing being captain of Wales has given me a fillip. As a kid I always wanted to be captain and go out first and I love it. Then again I'm not as quick tempered as I used to be. In the last two or three years I seem to have mellowed a lot and become a bit more relaxed about it all and that helps you enjoy the game more.

'I'm not as quick tempered as I used to be', says Terry Yorath, though he looks annoyed enough as he protests to the French referee over Peter Lorimer's disallowed goal for Leeds in the 1975 European Cup Final (below). Photo on facing page is of Trevor Hockey, sent off in the Poland–Wales World Cup game which says Yorath 'turned into a kicking match'.

39

TOP TWENTY

★ ★ ★ ★ ★ ★ ★ ★ ★

Another selection of World Stars presented by

BRIAN GLANVILLE

★ ★ ★

ARKADI ANDRIASSIAN (Ararat Erevan and Russia) Midfield inside-forward or centre-forward; beginning as the latter, though in his own, Hidegkuti-like, interpretation of the role. A native Armenian, born in 1947, Andriassian played a crucial part in Ararat's splendid Cup and League double of 1973, at the expense of the Moscow and Kiev 'monopolists', and figured in their commendable European Cup run of 1974/75, when they managed to beat but not eliminate Bayern Munich, the eventual victors. Fair haired and well built, he is a player of great versatility, well balanced, quick, strong, highly intelligent, able easily to beat a man; or to tackle him; alternatively, to knit his team skilfully together with his distribution. Greatly impressed the West Ham crowd when he captained Ararat against the Hammers in a Cupwinners' Cup tie in November, 1975; a match in which he seemed at one time or another to be filling with distinction almost every task on the field, save that of goalkeeper. A Russian international, member of the 1972 Olympic team, and capped against England in Moscow the following year, he has perhaps been a little unlucky in his international career. Latterly the hegemony of Dynamo Kiev has kept him out, despite his splendid form.

KEVIN BEATTIE (Ipswich Town and England) Turned up at Portman Road from his native Carlisle with sixpence in his pocket and a pair of boots in a

Photo (facing page) is of English international Kevin Beattie in action for Ipswich Town and (above) Russian star, Arkadi Andriassian.

brown paper parcel. Ipswich kept him and found they had a defensive left-half of immense potential, strong in the air and on the ground with a fine left foot, a crunching tackle, always ready besides to seek goals with either foot or head. Todd's excellence kept him out of his natural position in the England team, but late in season 1974/75 Don Revie decided to bring him in as a left-back; a position in which he enterprisingly headed a goal at Wembley against Scotland. Red haired, powerfully built, with a coolly precocious temperament on the field, he had one lapse that season off it, when he failed to turn up for an international game and went home to Carlisle instead. Revie generously forgave him.

MAURO BELLUGI (Bologna and Italy) A Tuscan, born at Buonconvento, near the exquisite city of Siena, on February 2, 1950, Bellugi was spotted, signed and brought to Milan by Internazionale, originally as a quick, forceful right-back. The man to man marking prevalent in Italian football made it easy enough for him to switch in due

Mauro Bellugi (photo left) heads clear for Italy against Holland, and above, Archie Gemmill in a typical action shot.

course to centre-half, especially as, though he's not very big, he is dominating in the air. He made his debut for Inter in the League at 19 in September, 1969, at Palermo. Three years later he was at right-back in their European Cup Final team, overwhelmed in Rotterdam by Ajax. His first cap came later in 1972 as left-back against Luxembourg in a World Cup game. He played steadily for the international team until 14 November 1973 when he helped it to beat England in London for the first time ever; then he fell out of favour and played no part in the 1974 World Cup. To add insult to injury, Inter sold him to Bologna and, a good Tuscan, he did not mince his words or hide his spleen. In Emilia he regained both his form and a place in the international side. You may say he has had the last laugh; or so it seems.

ARCHIE GEMMILL (Derby County and Scotland) Another of those stones that the builder kept scandalously rejecting. Just how Scotland could ignore Gemmill for the best (or worst) part of three years, before bringing him back as a late and splendid replacement against Denmark in October, 1975, one will never know. He could have been of immense use to them in the 1974 World Cup with his fearless running, his boundless stamina, his fine control, his distinguished passing. A traditional Scottish inside-forward in his lack of size, his close control, he is anything but traditional in the pace at which he does it all. To this extent he reminds one of Billy Steel. Born in Paisley, he joined the local club, St. Mirren, and crossed the border when Preston North End signed him in season 1967/68, when he made 29 Second Division appearances. Brian Clough brought him to Derby, where he was a major figure in their Championship season of 1971/72, adding a further medal when Derby repeated the feat in 1975. He has also had many fine games for them in the European Cup, though a highly doubtful booking and consequent suspension put him out of Derby's return semi-final against Juventus in 1973. Perhaps his performance against Real Madrid in that competition at the Baseball Ground in October, 1975 was the best that he has ever given.

REINHARD HÄFNER (Dynamo Dresden and East Germany) East German football slipped into the doldrums after the 1974 World Cup, but the performance of Häfner in midfield for club and country give hope for the future. Born on February 2, 1952 at Jonneberg in Thuringia, Häfner joined Dynamo Dresden at the age of 17, and is still studying to become a physical education teacher at Dresden University. Dark, solidly built in the legs, tireless on the field, he is an inside-forward in the old W formation mould, capable of making bullets for others, winning and retrieving the ball, shooting powerfully himself. He feels that his best years lie ahead of him: 'With time comes stamina . . . and I'm rather slight. For me, weight isn't the enemy.' His ambition is eventually to manage a football club. Meanwhile life, he admits, has been 'killing', by virtue of the double demands made by football and his university course. He appears to have survived them pretty well.

ALAN HUNTER (Ipswich Town and Northern Ireland) It took this strongly built, determined, dominating centre-half a surprisingly long time and a circuitous route to establish himself as an

Reinhard Häfner (photo left) and above, Alan Hunter closes on Leeds' Allan Clarke.

international, First Division footballer. Born in a tiny Ulster village in County Tyrone, brother of another Irish international, he was told by a female teacher that he'd 'end up emptying dustbins'. Leeds United were scarcely more encouraging when he had a trial with them at 19; they turned him down without even putting him into a practice game. But at Coleraine, Bertie Peacock turned him into a centre-half, and he came to England as a Third Division player; six years' hard, first with Oldham, then with Blackburn. In May, 1971, three outstanding games in the British Championship for Northern Ireland showed his potential at last—'I knew I had nothing to lose, I think I had everything to gain'— and soon Ipswich moved in, paying £100,000 for him. He's had his ups and downs at Portman Road, several times asking to be transferred. But he's been the prop of their defence; always in the right place, and a not infrequent, aerial presence in the opposing penalty box.

BRIAN LITTLE (Aston Villa and England)

Little's remarkable first twenty minutes for England, at Wembley against Wales, in May, 1975, constituted one of the finest debuts a forward can ever have made for his country. 22 years old, still a

Second Division player untried in international football, he galvanised an England team which looked well on the way to defeat by Wales, and with his fine left footed centre made the equaliser. His surprising 'reward' was promptly to be dropped; a disappointment compounded when, early in the new season, a cartilage operation put him out of the game for many weeks. A modest young man for all his success, his many decisive goals, Little has publicly said that he tends to lose concentration, paying tribute to the amount of help given him in the Villa attack by the promptings and solid physical presence of Leonard. One of two footballing brothers, Little is a Durham man, introduced by a scout who'd watched him since he was 13 and still believes him essentially an inside-forward. Small at 5-7½ and just over 10 stone, he makes up for that with his acceleration, courage, quick turn and nose for goal.

JOHN MAHONEY (Stoke City and Wales)

After Mahoney had played yet another splendid and decisive game in midfield for Wales, against Austria at Wrexham, thus qualifying them for the Nations Cup quarter-finals, in November, 1975, people said one didn't see the best of him with Stoke. The going theory was that Mahoney was inhibited

Brian Little, on the left, and above John Mahoney in action.

by the presence beside him of Alan Hudson. This may be true, though football history is full of distinguished Welshmen who played much better for their country than for their club. Standing 5–7½ and weighing about 11 stone, Mahoney is a swift, energetic, highly active midfield player, clever on the ball, a nice distributor, forceful in the tackle. Stoke signed him from Crewe Alexandra as long ago as season 1966/67, and he jumped straight from the Fourth to the First Division as an inside-forward, having made but a single League appearance for Crewe the season before. It took him a surprisingly long time to consolidate a place in the Welsh international side. He was capped against England in season 1967/68, but not for another five years did he become a regular player. Since Ivor Allchurch, there has surely been no better Welsh inside-forward; if the old nomenclature can be forgiven.

MARIAN MASNY (Slovan Bratislava and Czechoslovakia) A natural right winger with a splendid swerve outside the back, the ability to go to the line and cross, and considerable versatility beside, Masny will long be remembered by English players. He it was who 'roasted' Gillard and set up Czechoslovakia's winning goal against England on his home pitch in October 1975 in the Nations Cup; having been considerably involved with the first goal, too. Still only 25 at the time, the future of this elegant player seemed considerable. He combined especially well for club and country with the fair haired Slovan right-back, Pivarnik.

NENE (Benfica and Portugal) Though he missed a couple of very good chances for Portugal against England in Lisbon in November 1975, and a vital penalty a week earlier against the Czechs in Oporto, Nene remains one of the best Portuguese strikers of the moment. Born on November 20, 1949, he made a couple of Under 23 appearances against England and has gone on to win well over 20 full international caps, representing his country in the Nations and World Cup qualifying matches. He has also scored frequently in Benfica's triumphs in the Portuguese League; a fast, originally right side, player, who now plays more for Portugal as a centre-forward, swift off the mark with a strong right footed shot.

VLADIMIR ONISHENKO (Dynamo Kiev and Russia) Though this greatly gifted striker has

Marian Masny (dark shirt, left) evades Andersson (Sweden), and Vladimir Onishenko (above).

45

been a salient figure in Dynamo Kiev's success—not to mention Dynamo Kiev alias the Russian international team—it was with Zarja Voroshilovgrad that he made his name. He helped these doughty outsiders to win the Russian Championship, and played for Russia on the left wing in the Final of the European Nations Cup in Brussels in 1972. Born on April 26, 1949, he was transferred to Dynamo Kiev in 1973, though they already had a splendid left winger in Oleg Blokhin. There has, however, been no duplication, even though both players favour the left flank. They have dovetailed perfectly, never more so than in the European Cupwinners' Cup Final in Basel in May, 1975, when Onishenko scored two spectacular goals. One followed a dazzling individual run on the left, the other was a powerful shot from outside the penalty area.

CARLOS REXACH (Barcelona and Spain)

Tall, blond outside-right who has scored and made many goals for Barcelona in recent seasons. He got a hat trick against Feyenoord in the European Cup at Nou Camp in 1974, he scored from outside-left against Slovan Bratislava when they beat Barcelona in the Cupwinners' Cup Final in Basel in May, 1969. Perhaps Barcelona chose to overuse him in their European Cup run of 1974/75, both at Leeds, when Frankie Gray had the better of him, and in the semi-final return at Nou Camp, when there was something almost old fashioned about the way they fed him, hoping to exploit his fine, long centres. But he has been one of the best, most natural Spanish wingers of his day.

BRUCE RIOCH (Derby County and Scotland)

Though born in Aldershot, the son of a regular non-commissioned officer, Rioch qualified to play for Scotland because his father was a Scot. It finally happened in the British International Championship of 1975 in May, when he celebrated with a smashing, typically hit left footed goal against Wales, in Cardiff. Originally a centre-forward, he slipped through the hands of Chelsea, made a name with Luton Town, went to Aston Villa and became both their captain and a driving force in midfield; his brother played with him at Luton and Villa. Dave Mackay signed him for Derby County, and he

played a large part in their recapture of the First Division Championship in season 1974/75. Shows the adventurousness you would expect of a former striker, and his left footed dead ball kicks are specially formidable.

FRANCESCO ROCCA (Roma and Italy) A

lean, athletic, overlapping left-back of pace and technique, Rocca is a product of Roma, having been born at San Vito Romano, nearby, on August 2, 1954. He came through their youth team, and made his First Division (Serie A) debut on March 25, 1973, still an 18 year old, away to Milan; a hard match to begin in, and one which Roma lost 3–1. Two more appearances followed that season,

Bruce Rioch (photo above) in action, and (facing page), Francesco Rocca.

SANTILLANA (Carlos Alonso Gonzalez) (Real Madrid and Spain) His nickname of Santillana derives from the fact that he was born on August 23, 1952 at Santillana del Mar. He was signed by Barrere then Santander, missed by Barcelona, and was expensively transferred to Madrid in 1971; a tall centre-forward brave in the air, skilled on the ground. Kidney trouble in 1973 threatened his career, as did an eye injury later; he has often complained fiercely of the brutal treatment he receives from opposing centre-halves in Spain. But he has come through to lead the Spanish international attack and Real's with incision and distinction.

HUGO SOTIL (Barcelona and Peru) The return of this splendid little striker to the Barcelona attack in season 1975/76 made all the difference to Cruyff and the team. Sotil himself seemed none the worse for a season spent kicking his heels, Neeskens' arrival at Barcelona having rendered him one foreigner too many to play. In the season before he had combined beautifully and fruitfully with Cruyff, enabling Barcelona to have their magnificent long run in to the League Championship. He joined the Catalan club in 1973 from Deportivo Municipal of Lima, played 34 games for 11 goals. Played every World Cup game for Peru in the tournament of 1974 in Mexico when they reached the quarter finals; small, solid, beautifully balanced and adroit.

and in the following one he was a regular League team player, with 30 appearances. 1975 saw him consolidate his position in the international side, not least with an excellent performance in Warsaw, against Poland. A solid successor to Facchetti, even if he perhaps tends to cross where Facchetti would try to shoot.

DOMINIQUE ROCHETEAU (Saint Etienne and France) In season 1969/70, Rocheteau was picked for the final of a competition for young footballers, which took place in Paris at the Parc des Princes. He finished bottom out of the whole 22, but that very shrewd old scout Pierre Garonnaire of Saint Etienne had noticed him, signed him, and has never regretted it. By season 1975/76, now aged 20, Rocheteau was a young star on the right wing, forcing his way into both the French international and the Saint Etienne first teams. If he has faults they are merely the obverse of his virtues, a natural winger's propensity to hang on to the ball. Comes from a family which for years has raised oysters; that was to be his destiny, too, but he preferred to make football ... his oyster; and Garonnaire persuaded his father to let him.

JOHN TOSHACK (Liverpool and Wales) Six feet one inch tall with huge shoulders, Toshack is famous for the heading powers which won Liverpool the UEFA Cup of 1973 and Wales a place in the Nations Cup quarter-finals of 1976; but he is an undervalued player on the ground. Since Bob Paisley took over as Liverpool manager, he has worked hard on his all round game, and with success. A once clumsy forward has become dangerous and sometimes surprisingly elusive. Cardiff born, Toshack joined Cardiff City from school, made his name and won international caps there, in 1968/69, joined Liverpool in 1970. Has had his spells out of the League team, but they have always been obliged to recall him. He is a particular terror against most continental defences, less used to dealing with such power in the air.

DAVE WATSON (Manchester City and England) Born in Nottingham, Watson is one of several footballing brothers and though he has done so well as England's centre-half, he was something of a late developer. He began with Notts County who sold him to Rotherham. Thence he moved to Sunderland—a centre-half who often played at centre-forward—settled at Roker and made his name. He was their indomitable centre-half in the Cup Final of 1973 when they beat Leeds United. The following year he was called up by England to solve a difficult problem at centre-half, caused by injury to Roy McFarland. Watson played splendidly, with strength, confidence, mobility and poise on England's 1974 European tour, and even when McFarland returned to football in 1975, it was nip and tuck between them for the international position. That summer, Watson, unhappy by now at Sunderland, had been transferred for a huge fee to Manchester City.

WLADYSLAW ZMUDA (Slask Wroclaw and Poland) The defensive revelation of the 1974 World Cup, when Poland brought him in as a 20 year old and he played impeccably in every game, ending with a third place medal. Afterwards he asked for a transfer to Slask, since his girl friend lived in Wroclaw, from Gwardia Warsaw. He was suspended for a year but amnestied in the Spring, when the Poles decided they needed this tall, strong, cool centre-back to play against Italy.

Dave Watson (below) in action during an England training session with Mike Channon getting a very close view of the ball.

WE ARE NOT RUTHLESS ENOUGH AT QUEENS PARK RANGERS

By Eire International

DON GIVENS

• • •

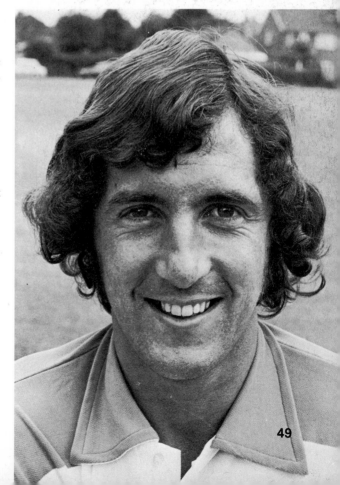

ALTHOUGH we still have a few problems if we are to stay amongst the leading contenders for the game's top honours, the current team is surely the best that Q.P.R. have ever had. This opinion is underlined by the fact that many uncommitted fans think we are the most attractive team in the country from the viewpoint of entertaining, attacking football.

In the league we had a couple of patches when we didn't get many goals for a few weeks and that cost us dearly. But I think our real problem was underlined by the manner in which we went out of the FA Cup to Newcastle. In the first leg at Shepherds Bush we didn't play particularly well.

We play too much football, in attack and defence, says Don Givens, pictured on the right.

49

I thought we were the better side but didn't do enough in attack to win. But in the replay we played better than we had for weeks, missed a penalty and hit two shots against the posts to lose 2–1 on a penalty.

For me, this game underlined what is our present failing: we are simply not ruthless enough and this goes right throughout the whole side. In attack we don't take enough of the chances we create, and in defence, though the back four were really tremendous last season we give away vital goals. This I believe is because we try to play too much football.

Without losing any of our appeal we must face the fact that there are times in defence when you are under pressure in your own danger zone and a big kick into the stand is the best answer. Not all the time of course, generally we should go on playing our way out of defence but we haven't yet learned to pick out the times when the answer is to thump the ball out.

I have taken penalties myself, earlier in my career but you are on a hiding to nothing with each one.

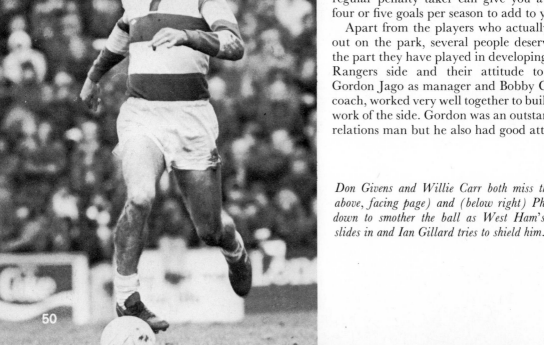

England winger Dave Thomas in a typical pose with the ball at his feet (left) and above, Don Masson says 'How about that' after scoring one of his two goals against Birmingham City last season.

The only good thing is that as a striker, being the regular penalty taker can give you a start of say four or five goals per season to add to your tally.

Apart from the players who actually do the job out on the park, several people deserve credit for the part they have played in developing the current Rangers side and their attitude to the game. Gordon Jago as manager and Bobby Campbell his coach, worked very well together to build the framework of the side. Gordon was an outstanding public relations man but he also had good attacking ideas

Don Givens and Willie Carr both miss the ball (photo above, facing page) and (below right) Phil Parkes goes down to smother the ball as West Ham's Pat Holland slides in and Ian Gillard tries to shield him.

51

about the game and all the players he bought had an attacking bent.

Bobby was a really terrific motivator and very popular but Terry Venables our former captain must be mentioned too. He worked very closely with Gordon and Bobby on our style of play and was instrumental in first getting it going.

Then came Dave Sexton with his superb knowledge of the game which is second to none. Utterly dedicated to football and a terrific fellow, he had problems before he came to us but none at all at Rangers.

My part in it all is to get goals, but though I wear the number 11 shirt and did play out wide when I first joined Rangers from Luton, I am now a central striker.

I was a winger when I joined Manchester United straight from school but I didn't quite measure up to their standard. They gave me a spell in midfield but after four years with them they transferred me to Luton for £15,000. I had one full season for Luton playing in midfield but I always preferred playing up front.

Luton let me go to Rangers for £38,000 in June 1971. This was before Stan Bowles or Dave Thomas joined the club and I was the only player at that time to have played out wide, playing on either wing for Manchester United, so that was where they played me.

It isn't easy, scoring goals today, for apart from the tight marking and quick tackling there are an awful lot of good defenders about. Colin Todd is the most difficult man I've faced—reading the

Gordon McQueen, seen below in action for Scotland against England at Wembley is a very difficult man to beat—quick, strong and specially good in the air, says Don Givens.

game very well and so quick to recover if you do beat him.

Gordon McQueen of Leeds is another difficult man to get the better of. He's quick and a strong lad all round but specially good in the air. Then there's Kevin Beattie of Ipswich who is almost as good as Todd defensively though he is not quite so good when it comes to distributing the ball once he's won it.

For goalkeepers I rate our own Phil Parkes very highly. He had a great time last season but the best 'keeper I've played against, indeed the best I've seen is Tottenham's Pat Jennings.

In the international sense I've never played in any of the big club competitions but I earned my 30th cap for the Republic of Ireland last autumn and hope to get a few more. We have quite a useful side now and might well have reached the quarter

Supremely gifted Stan Bowles (photo right) raises his arms in triumph after scoring the winning goal against Burnley, and, below, manager Dave Sexton explains a point during a coaching session.

finals of the European championship if we'd been drawn in an easier group without the Russians.

Eire's team improved tremendously when Johnny Giles took over as player-manager. Before that, everything was a bit haphazard, particularly the pre-match preparations and travelling. At that time you simply turned up the day before the game and were introduced to the other players who were sometimes complete strangers.

Johnny Giles changed all that and we are much more professional now. We get together two or three times a year in addition to meeting for matches and I'm sure this has been a big factor in our improved results.

My big day was of course the 4–0 win over Turkey at Dalymount Park, Dublin, last year. I didn't play significantly better than in other games but I was lucky enough to score all four goals. It was just one of those days. I had about five chances and four of them went in. On an average day you get five or six chances and manage to put one away and think you are doing well.

Until last year I thought that the Brazilian side we met in 1970 was the best national side I'd seen. We played Brazil in a friendly two or three weeks before the Mexico World Cup which Brazil won. Pelé didn't play against us but I thought they had a really good side with Rivelino standing out as the star.

Then in the European championship we fell foul of the Russians in 1975. We had beaten Russia 3–0 in Dublin at the start of the competition and really fancied our chances after that. Then the Russian FA, decided to field the complete Dynamo Kiev team as their national side and they turned out to be the best team I've ever seen, better even than Brazil.

We only lost 2–1 in Kiev, shortly after Dynamo had won the European Cupwinners Cup, but in the first half they played a brand of football that was by far the best I've ever seen, better even than Manchester United's first team when I was with them!

They really were out of this world and I'm sure they'll prove themselves to be a truly outstanding team. They had quite a few brilliant individuals but their overall team work was so simple and their passing so accurate we just couldn't get the ball. They played to an ordinary 4–3–3 formation but their six attacking players, the middle three and the front three, were all outstanding; classy with the ball but really working hard too and playing as a team.

Oleg Blokhin who was voted European Footballer of the Year for 1975 was their best individual, skilful and so quick, but Vladimir Muntjan in midfield and their captain Victor Kolotov were not far behind him in class and the overall effect was terrific. I'm sure we'll be hearing a lot more about them in the next two or three years.

Mick Leach and David Webb (background) reinforce the attack for a corner against Sheffield United, foiled by goalkeeper Jim Brown (photo below) and pictured right (facing page) Frank McLintock in trouble with the referee.

REAL MADRID'S ARGENTINIAN STAR

Says

THE SPANISH GAME IS TOUGHER THAN IN ARGENTINA

• • • • • • • by • • • • • • • •
ROBERTO MARTINEZ

◆ ◆ ◆ ◆

FOR the majority of South American players, certainly those in Argentina and Uruguay, European football is a kind of Mecca. For one thing, the money is better; bigger salaries and for key games some very big bonuses indeed, but this is only when you are successful with one of the great clubs.

It is true that Argentinian and Uruguayan clubs do not always respect the players contracts. Every now and again one hears of a club that is several months behind in paying their players, but you

In action (left) Roberto Martinez jumps into the air to control the ball with his thigh and (photo right) Real Madrid captain 'Pirri'.

57

only hear of this when the players threaten to strike and the story gets into the newspapers.

But it isn't only money that attracts us to Europe. Inevitably, being Spanish-speaking, most Argentinians join clubs in Spain as I did, and there lies the opportunity to prove yourself as a professional player. Amongst the top teams in Europe everything is better organised but the most important thing I think is that there can be no doubt that the game in Europe is the highest standard in the world. To prove yourself in European football is the real challenge.

In my case it is true that I first joined a club of relatively inferior standing but I have no regrets about that. It might have been very different for before I was transferred to RCD Espanol, I was offered a trial with their giant neighbours FC Barcelona. Unfortunately I was injured at the time

Real Madrid midfield player Manuel Velazquez, a veteran of the 1966 European Cup success (below) and photo right, in his days in Germany, Gunter Netzer, 'a world figure' says Roberto Martinez.

Barcelona's representatives visited Buenos Aires and missed that chance.

Thirty years old now, I was born in Mendoza, Argentina in 1946 and my first club was a Second Division team, Nueva Mexicana. In that first season as a part-time professional I attracted the attention of my local First Division club, Huracan of Mendoza and was transferred to them.

I spent only one season with each of my Argentinian clubs, being transferred at the end of each season and always taking a step up the ladder. From Huracan—not to be confused with the Huracan

Derby County's Archie Gemmill falls to a tackle from Del Bosque (photo above right) and below right, Grosso and goalkeeper Miguel Angel combine to thwart Derby's Francis Lee.

of Buenos Aires, I joined Union CF, of Santa Fé and finally reached the big league in Buenos Aires where I played for Banfield FC.

Buenos Aires swarms with scouts who have contacts with Spanish clubs and I was approached by several agents. I don't know what they get for finding a player and it's none of my business anyway. The fact is they exist and several of them approached me. One scout offered to fix me up with a trial with FC Barcelona but as I said when the representative of Barcelona arrived, I was injured and he couldn't see me play.

I began to think that perhaps I had missed my chance when another scout came to me and asked if I would be interested in joining Espanol. I didn't need asking twice and after I had undergone some physical tests and a medical examination, Banfield agreed to the move and I signed. I think the transfer fee Banfield received was around £20,000 but I have no idea what the scout received. All I know is that I was given a signing-on bonus of £2,250 and quite a good contract. I was more than satisfied.

Of course I realised that Espanol have never been a club that is widely known in international circles, but I joined them hoping that it would enable me to improve my play, and with luck I might attract a bigger club. That was exactly how it worked out, for luckily I had some good games for Espanol and Real Madrid signed me. Playing on the left wing I scored 16 league goals in my first season, 1974–75, when Real Madrid won the championship and I had achieved my ambition.

There were many things that were strange to me when I first arrived in Spain. The game in Spain is generally tougher than in Argentina—but the referees also exercise better control. The Spaniards play to win, and they play hard because there are big bonuses for winning. But I was pleasantly surprised to find also that the players seem to have a mutual respect for each other as professionals and as a result the standard of sportsmanship is also higher than in Argentina.

I also had to adjust to the faster and different style of play in Spain. There were many football problems that had to be overcome and I owe a great deal to Jose Santamaria, the Espanol manager who was formerly the centre back of Real Madrid and Uruguay. He was like a football father to me

Right winger Amancio (photo above) is now 36 years old but still an automatic first choice. When he is unfit, Roberto Martinez, naturally right-footed, switches from the left wing, getting goals from either flank.

and it is largely due to him that I was successful in Spain.

Though I joined Espanol hoping to move on to a bigger club, when the chance came I didn't really want to leave them. There is a very good spirit within the club and I was very happy with them. They are a small club, constantly living in the shadows of their rich and powerful neighbours FC Barcelona. They are growing slowly, but they lack the financial backing that clubs like Real Madrid and FC Barcelona have and so they continually have to transfer players to maintain economic stability. Someone had to go and Real Madrid made what was presumably a good offer for me, so I went.

Of course I earn more with Real Madrid and settled down very quickly. They had a new manager at the time I moved, the Yugoslav Miljan Miljanic who is very much like Santamaria in many ways. He really knows the game and proved himself to the players and the club in his first season.

Playing for Real Madrid is almost a unique experience because of their past. They are the team everyone wants to beat and particularly in Spanish league games it is like playing in a Cup Final every week. Yet strangely, though we are aware of a special sense of responsibility there is no real pressure on us. This I think is because the players and the manager get on so well together.

'Argentina can be a real force in the 1978 World Cup' says Martinez (below). Stars are constantly emerging there and in Buenos Aires they still say that every boy is born with a football under his arm.

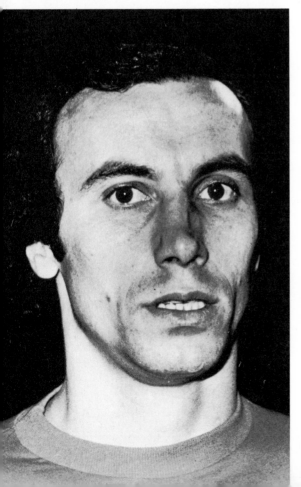

Playing with World Class players like Paul Breitner and Gunter Netzer is a real pleasure. They are truly real figures in world football and a benefit to the game and all around them. Then we have some very good Spanish players too like Pirri and Santillana the centre forward with whom I share the striking role.

Real are a special kind of club. They respect the contracts of the players meticulously and always treat the players well as individuals. And of course their fans have a great passion for the club and the game.

Unfortunately, I have been the subject, among others, of some very bitter attacks by some Spanish clubs and some sections of the press. I played for Spain after acquiring Spanish nationality, in the 1974 World Cup qualifying round and later against Denmark and Scotland in the 1976 European championship. Then the rumours began to fly and I had a very difficult time.

From my point of view the facts are clear. Both my parents were born in Argentina but through grandparents on both sides of the family, I am of Spanish descent. Under Spanish law there is no difficulty and when I asked for Spanish nationality in 1972 there were no problems.

I had to present all my papers, birth certificate, passport etc., and swear an oath. Everything was in order and I acquired dual nationality.

I believe it was not a personal attack on me but a way for some people to get at Real Madrid. Real have thousands of big fans but they also have many great enemies who are jealous of the club's success. The accusations made against me, were I believe made by enemies of Real Madrid—I was merely the instrument they used to attack the club. After all, no one said a word when I first played for Spain —but at that time I was with little Espanol!

Having played for Spain I cannot play for Argentina now whatever happens but I am sure they will do really well in the 1978 World Cup. I know an awful lot of players have emigrated to Europe, but the game is a real passion in Argentina and figures are always emerging as individuals. There are problems in the field of organisation but these can be overcome and they still say in Buenos Aires that every Argentinian boy is born with a football under his arm.

SUNDERLAND
MA

CAN MATCH
NCHESTER UNITED
FOR GATES

<table>
<tr><td>by</td></tr>
<tr><td>Sunderland F.C. star</td></tr>
<tr><td>**TONY TOWERS**</td></tr>
</table>

SUNDERLAND supporters in my opinion are amongst the best in the country, even on a par with Manchester United's. Football has long traditions up here in the North-East and it was not really so long ago that Sunderland were one of the top dogs in English football.

Tradition dies hard and some idea of the locals enthusiasm for the game can be gauged from the fact that in the season that Sunderland were relegated to the Second Division their home attendances averaged 44,000.

Tony Towers (photo left) roars a command to a team mate. On the right is Towers' club mate Tom Finney, a player with an illustrious name who, unlike the Preston 'plumber', plays for Northern Ireland.

Even in Division II, Sunderland pull in a regular 30,000 which is really good for you have to consider that not many fans make the long journey up north from places like Plymouth and Portsmouth so what it means is that all the 30,000 are Sunderland fans. Back in the top class, Sunderland will be pulling in a regular 50,000 with no trouble.

Our fans at Roker Park are also amongst the most discerning spectators who come to be entertained as well as see their team win. You can't kid anyone at Roker when you play badly!

But having been in Division II for a while and missing promotion so narrowly and disappointingly in the last two seasons, I thought I felt a slight

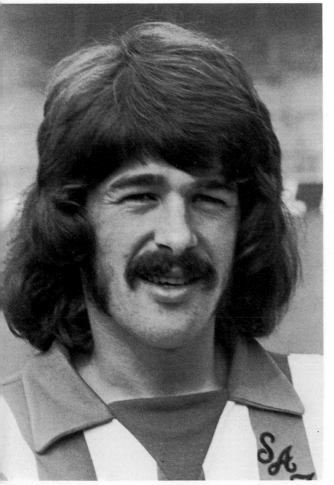

change last season in 1975–76. Though they want to enjoy their football and see the clever stuff, there developed an underlying frustration which is easily understandable—their position shifted slightly to one of . . . 'play the clever stuff if you can, but whatever happens let us keep on winning and get back into the First Division!'

When I joined Sunderland from Manchester City I really thought Sunderland would very quickly return to the top class. After winning the FA Cup, beating Leeds at Wembley, they obviously had a good side and a great spirit within the team. But things went wrong, really because we gave away silly goals against some of the lesser teams and consequently dropped vital points.

Bobby Kerr (photo left) has been one of Sunderland's most consistent players. Photo above, is Roy Greenwood, a left winger whom Sunderland manager, Bob Stokoe, signed from Hull City after Billy Hughes was seriously injured last season.

For example we were leading Fulham 1–0 two seasons back but gave away two goals and lost 2–1 at home. Then we dropped two points in drawn games with Oldham, drawing away but starting the return match at Roker as if we were going to walk it. Leading 2–0 we let Oldham back in the game with another silly goal and they ended up drawing 2–2 and taking a point away from us.

You can afford the occasional lapse if you are a First Division club and only need to stay up. But when you are going for promotion—and preferably by being champions—you just cannot afford to drop silly points. I have no doubt that it is a lot more difficult to get up out of Division II than it is to stay

up in Division I.

In the First Division a good start is enough to get you well away from the relegation zone and then you gain time. Time to bring on youngsters and maybe sign a big name player to strengthen the team and enlarge your first team squad. Going

The big clubs of the North-East are all traditionally First Division. With Newcastle Utd., regaining their Cup traditions last season and Middlesbrough re-established in the top class, Sunderland's return will restore the tradition. Pictured below is Middlesbrough 'keeper Jim Platt saving from Trevor Whymark of Ipswich Town.

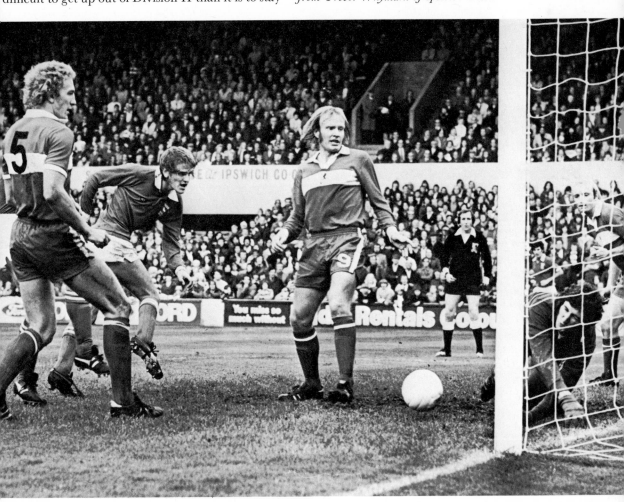

orderly fashion to defend their goal and this gives you time to look up when you have the ball and make a useful pass.

Last season I thought we had a better balanced side than in the previous campaign. For one thing we signed 'Pop' Robson who you can always rely on to get goals and when right winger Billy Hughes got injured, our manager Bob Stokoe went to Hull for Roy Greenwood. He is a left winger who I am sure will prove to be a very good buy. With Hughes back in action, we had two really good wingers.

Then of course we brought in young Joe Bolton at left back who is a very good player—a future cap unless I am very much mistaken.

for promotion you can't afford to give good young reserves a few games to let them settle down in case it costs you valuable points that you will never be able to make up.

Coming from the First Division as I did, you quickly realise that Second Division football is played at a much more hectic pace. Apart from the handful of sides at the top of the Second Division, it is pretty well a kick and rush type game that predominates. Players fly about all over the place with someone biting at your heels every time you get the ball.

In the First Division you get more time and space for in the top class the marking and tackling only get really tight when you get close to the enemy penalty area. The tendency is to fall back in an

Tony Towers is not the only Sunderland player with First Division experience. Bryan 'Pop' Robson (photo above), 'who', says Towers, 'you can always rely on for goals' was previously with Newcastle and West Ham, while Bobby Moncur (photo right) was the key man in Newcastle's defence for several seasons.

Joe Bolton (photo right) claimed a regular place at left back for Sunderland last season and, says Tony Towers, is a near certainty to get caps.

As a First Division player I think my personal chances of getting into the England team will be improved. I played for England Schoolboys; the England Youth team, and also captained the Under 23 side. I got as far as a place in the full England squad and was substitute too so I wasn't far away. Bearing in mind that I will be only 26 at the time of the 1978 World Cup, I think it's a fair bet that I'll get a chance to show what I can do for England have obviously got to build a new side that will be young enough for 1978. Anyway, I am optimistic.

Although I joined Sunderland after their FA Cup Final win I have already been to Wembley once— with Manchester City. That was a big thrill, playing in the League Cup Final but we lost 2–1 to Wolves which gave it a disappointing end.

Playing at Wembley is always something special to a professional footballer—but I hope there'll be more opportunities in the future. In any case I got off to a very good start in my career, helping Manchester City to win the European Cupwinners Cup in 1970. We beat the Polish Cup Winners of the time, Gornik Zabrze in the final when I was only 17 and though I'm not usually a goal scorer I was lucky enough to get a vital one on the way to that final.

Playing against the Portuguese side Academica, we drew 0–0 away and then at home it was still 0–0 at the end of normal time. The tie went into an extra thirty minutes and with only a minute of extra time left I went upfield and got the winner to take us into the semi finals.

I get one or two goals now and again but I'm not what you would call a goalscorer, or even an attacking player. I started with Manchester City playing an up and down game in midfield, playing on the left hand side but later I switched into the middle of the back four. Then Malcolm Allison signed Rodney Marsh from Queens Park Rangers and as Malcolm told me at the time, being the youngest member of the side I had to give up my place to make room for him. 'But' he said, 'if any-

one did not play well I would be back in the team' and the very next week I took over temporarily from Mike Doyle and stayed in the side until Ron Saunders arrived as the new manager.

All in all things worked out very well for me though I didn't want to leave Maine Road and I was a bit too young to understand what transfers were all about. Luckily for me I was transferred to a good club and settled down very quickly at Roker Park. They are all nice people here and in a happy atmosphere I felt at home right away. Now all I want is to be part of a successful Sunderland set-up and with a bit of luck get a chance to earn a regular place in the England team.

AJAX ARE ON

Ruud Geels (portrait above) and right, in action against Austria.

THE UPGRADE AGAIN

AGAIN

By

RUUD GEELS

AJAX AND HOLLAND STRIKER

coming out of goal, for instance to deal with high crosses. We didn't play on that, but it probably made things that much easier for me. The decisive factor that day was that Ajax played really superbly in attack with all the forwards in top form and inter-changing positions so often that the Feyenoord defenders didn't know who to mark. I think that was the real key, so I owe most to my colleagues play that made it possible.

I have twice scored more than five in one game. In my early days playing for the professional youth team of Telstar, my first club, I scored seven goals in an 11–0 win over a team called Gooiland. Then in my time with one of the top Belgian clubs FC

AS A professional footballer and a striker it's always a great feeling when you come off the pitch having scored five goals. But when I got five against Feyenoord last season for Ajax it was really enormous.

For one thing, I was once a Feyenoord player myself—and you always like to do well against your old club—but Feyenoord's reputation and even now, high standing in Dutch football makes it even more impressive. To get five against an ordinary team like Telstar or Excelsior is one thing, but Feyenoord? I could hardly believe it.

The Feyenoord 'keeper Eddy Treytel I knew of old, having played with him often. He is a very good goalkeeper, one of the three 'keepers in the Dutch 1974 World Cup 22, but although he's very good saving shots on the line, he's not so good at

Much of the strength of the famed Ajax attack has always come from their full backs, Wim Suurbier (portrait above) and Ruud Krol seen after scoring (photo right) in a league match against Go Ahead FC.

Bruges, I got six goals against PSV Eindhoven though that was only a friendly match.

A good win over Feyenoord is always nice of course, specially when you know the rivalry between Ajax (Amsterdam) and Feyenoord (Rotterdam) but you have to be realistic. It was one of Ajax's best performances of the season. In the first half of last season for example we had only one defeat but what a hiding that was. We were away to the reigning champions PSV and we got well beaten by six goals to two.

It was quite early in the season and the Ajax team was in the process of rebuilding. Most of the well known stars had gone and it was a critical match. We went onto the pitch with good intentions but I think each of us was secretly expecting to be beaten and out on the field everything went wrong.

PSV are a very good team, really grandiose and their players are still young. They have some out-standing individuals and having been together for several years play very well together. I'm sure they have a big future, and perhaps even by the time this article is published they will already have proved themselves in Europe.

Certainly PSV have an outstanding team, but that defeat marked the turning point for Ajax and I'm sure they will not get another chance to put six goals past us. We are on the upgrade once again.

This doesn't mean that I think Ajax are going to be a great side again by European standards. It's much too early for that. The way back is a long one and it will not be easy to reach the standard of Ajax when they had players like Cruyff and

Flashback to Ajax's last visit to London. Ray Kennedy (dark shirt), then with Arsenal, looks on with moustached Barry Hulshoff while Suurbier heads clear.

71

Scenes from the glory days of Ajax. Above, Johnny Rep skates past two Bayern München defenders and facing page (upper photo) Arie Haan in a heading duel with CSKA (Bulgaria) striker Georgi Denev while Johan Neeskens (4) and Barry Hulshoff (3) look on. Lower picture shows Atanas Michaelov heading a goal for CSKA with, from left to right, Suurbier, Neeskens, Denev and Hulshoff all spectators.

Neeskens. But I am optimistic about our future. We have a good team with some very good players, but first we have to win the Dutch championship. After that, we shall see.

Here in Holland the championship is dominated by three or four clubs. Every team plays a slightly different kind of football though the differences are not as great as in England. But when the leading clubs like Ajax, PSV, FC Twente and of course Feyenoord, play against a lesser club there are a lot of teams that play with very defensive tactics.

Rinus Michels, seen on left eating a 1974 World Cup breakfast is the man who built the Super-Ajax and is now back in Amsterdam after his stint in Spain.

Many people seem to expect Holland to do very well again in the 1978 World Cup. But it's time England had a good team again and of course new faces are emerging in other countries too. Teams that were not so good in 1974 can find a few new, outstanding players and be really good. That's why I'm a bit cautious about Holland's chances.

Rinus Michels who is now back as the coach of Ajax was the man behind Holland's 1974 success. All the Ajax players have tremendous respect for him and his obvious deep understanding of the game. Undoubtedly he was the man who was responsible for creating the great Ajax team of the past. As far as I am concerned I don't really know him well enough yet but I shall always be grateful to him for choosing me for the Dutch 1974 squad, even though I was playing in Belgium at the time.

Although I've still got a few good years ahead of me I am already quite well travelled in football. My first club was Telstar, a First Division team near Haarlem where I was born in July, 1948. After six months in their Youth team I was promoted to the First XI and then Feyenoord made an offer for me and I signed. I was four years in Rotterdam, then moved for two seasons to another Dutch club, Go Ahead Eagles of Deventer and at that time the Belgian club, FC Bruges signed me.

I had a three year contract with Bruges but before it was up, Ajax wanted to sign me. FC Bruges found themselves in a difficult position after spending more than £½ million on players. They needed to transfer someone and Ajax made a big offer for me. I didn't specially want to join Ajax but Bruges needed the money so I went. It was a good move for Bruges financially, and as it turned out a good move for me too. In my first season I was the top scorer in Holland and the second highest scorer in European league football too.

Then of course my move to Ajax opened the door to the Dutch national team. I had played for Holland at Youth international level and also in the Under

In Holland it's always one of the top four teams that win the championship. That's what I like about English football because at the start of the season it's wide open. Almost anyone can take the title and nearly anyone can be relegated.

Because so many teams adopt defensive tactics in Holland I think there are more good matches in England, at least that's the impression I have from the games I have seen on television. I've seen a lot of good players with English clubs and there must be many more that I don't know. That's why I feel it must be possible to build a good English national team and I can't understand what has gone wrong.

23 side but in 1975 I got my first full cap . . . on the right wing against Poland. I was always a central striker till then but it was Dutch national team manager George Knobel's idea to play me on the wing against Poland in Amsterdam.

For Ajax I line up on the right wing but that's only on paper. Really I play in the centre, but for Holland I tried to play like a real winger. I found it was not too difficult, probably because on the wing there is more space and you are not so tightly marked. As a winger you have the left back on you, but at centre forward you nearly always have two men to beat, the stopper marking you and the free back or *libero* close behind him.

In my time with Feyenoord they had plenty of really good forwards including the Swedish international centre forward Ove Kindvall who scored the winning goal for them when they won the

European Cup, beating Celtic 2–1 in the final in 1970. I was with them then but didn't play in the final.

Being only 17 when I joined Feyenoord I couldn't expect to be a regular first team player but in fact I played on average about 25 first team games per season in my 4 years with them. Kindvall was of course a high class player of fantastic value to Feyenoord. Speed was his biggest asset but I was fast too and though Kindvall scored a lot of goals he didn't seem to be very happy playing in the snow and ice and mud of the Dutch winter. In Sweden they never played in the winter and like most Scandinavian players he didn't seem to like it.

Nowadays of course the big Dutch player is Johan Cruyff, though it seems many people don't like him. In the beginning I think everybody saw him as crazy about money, a maniac. But I don't think it's true. He pays about half what he earns in taxes and a footballer's career is short so he has to think about money like all of us.

Ove Kindvall (below at the near post) scores a league goal for Feyenoord. Now a veteran, Kindvall is still playing in Sweden.

In my opinion he is, with Pelé, the best player the world ever had and I like him. To me he seems just a normal guy in spite of all the publicity he gets. Also he is always the first to help other players and as a man I like him too.

No one else I know has a better approach to coaches and officials of the FA, and if one of the other players gets into some difficulty with an official, Cruyff always intervenes and seems able to sort things out amicably.

Cruyff's biggest critics accuse him of not giving 100% sometimes but I don't agree. I've never seen it anyway. But when you think about it, football is like any other job and whether you work in an office or a factory there are surely some days when you just don't feel like work?

Here in Holland we have a much better transfer system than you have in England though I understand there are some changes coming in your regulations. I don't like the transfer system. It's too much like a slave trade, making the players feel like a cow on sale at a market. In Holland, unless you've signed a contract for some years it's always possible to get a transfer. Even then, if another club offers you better financial conditions all you have to do is appeal to a civil court and your club is ordered to transfer you.

That's a much fairer system and for the sake of my fellow professionals all over the world I'd like to see it operate everywhere.

MY WISH IS TO EMULATE BILLY McNEILL AND LEAD CELTIC TO SUCCESS IN EUROPE

Says **KENNY DALGLISH** of **CELTIC** and **SCOTLAND**

77

IT WAS the 27th of May, 1967 and I was sitting at home glued to the television. That day Celtic were playing Inter Milan in the final of the European Cup in Lisbon.

I don't think I'll ever forget the drama and excitement of that game when Celtic took on and beat the much-fancied Italians. And they did it with the kind of attractive, attacking and creative football which was a revelation to Europeans suffering from defensive Italian dominance.

With that game Celtic had arrived . . . the greatest club side in Europe and supreme in Scotland. Attacking open football was back in fashion.

And this was the team I was about to join, the club I was to captain only 8 years later.

Celtic manager Jock Stein was recognised as one of soccer's top tacticians in the world, and his backroom staff was second to none. His team, with players like McNeill, Murdoch and Gemmell, Johnstone and Lennox, had become household names.

What better way to start a professional career than to join the champions of Europe. For the honour of captaining Celtic is only equalled by being asked to play for them.

It was a year after that great final that I got my first game in the League, a match against Raith Rovers which we won 7–1. And playing alongside me were most of those 'Lisbon Lions'. At that time the first division in the Scottish League contained 18 teams.

And the so-called 'banker' win for Celtic wasn't as easy as it might have seemed. The weaker teams revelled in the atmosphere at Parkhead, or in front of the large travelling Celtic support at their home ground.

But it was clear that the set-up wasn't quite right . . . too many games were meaningless.

Kenny Dalglish (photo left) where he is most elusive—with the ball at his feet—and (above) Leeds United's Gordon McQueen, one of the few 'Anglos' who would be a unanimous choice for Scotland.

Now several changes have taken place in Scottish football in recent seasons, which should undoubtedly improve the standard of play in this country.

The arrival of the Premier League with its ten clubs has made teams more aware, and more cautious in their approach.

The gap between the top and bottom of the Premier League has never been closer ... to lose two points could mean a drop of three places. And with so few clubs in the running you can suddenly find yourself nudging the relegation zone.

But it has not meant a return to defensive football. For the clubs have gone all out for the points and we have had some tremendous matches.

The goal tally is up, and some of the missing fans are gradually being lured back to the grounds.

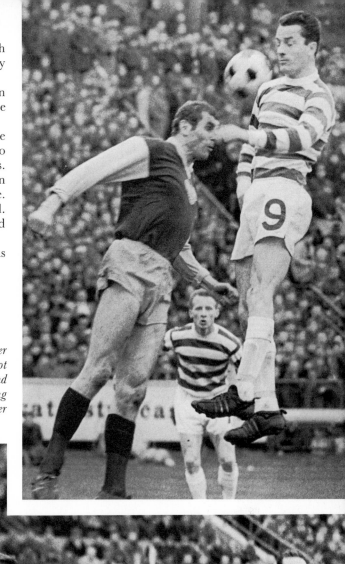

Flashback to Celtic's golden days in Europe's premier competition. Below, Billy McNeill goes upfield to try a shot at goal in an away 0–0 draw with Dukla Prague, and (photo right) another shot from the same game showing Steve Chalmers who later scored the winning goal v Inter in the 1967 Final.

Celtic's Danny McGrain (above) beats Kevin Keegan to the ball in the 1975 England–Scotland game at Wembley won surprisingly easily by England, 5–1.

It's important to remember too, that some of the best games have not involved the old firm of Rangers and Celtic.

My personal feeling, however, is that it may prove too much to play every other team four times. From the fans' point of view anyway. For if Premier League clubs are also drawn together in the League and Scottish cups as well that might mean six meetings.

Of course if their first game turns out a real cracker, then the crowds will still show up for the others.

But equally if the first tie is a stinker, and there are another four or five meetings inside six months still to come, then attracting sufficient paying customers could be a real problem.

I think I would like to see a twelve club Premier League, which would still retain the quality, while cutting the league clashes to two games against each team.

Another idea which might have financial benefit would be to seed the top clubs in the Scottish Cup. At least for the first round. For it could happen that only five clubs from the top division survive after the first round, and from both a monetary and a spectating point of view, this is hardly desirable.

Comparisons between Scottish and English league football are always being made and I must agree that the overall standard of the English First Division is very high. None of the games look easy. But Celtic have always fared well against English opposition both in friendly and competitive matches. It has to be admitted though that other Scottish clubs have had few answers to the strength in depth of English League clubs.

During my career there has been one other development in Scottish football which can only be for the good. Many young and enthusiastic managers have arrived who have a better understanding of the modern game and have introduced a new tactical approach.

For although clubs may have more to lose in our new league set-up, the rewards for success are greater, and, with young managers looking for success, the game has improved.

I would like to think that many of them were following Celtic's lead, following in the footsteps of a club whose main aim has always been to entertain, and above all not to enter any game with a negative approach.

This new breed of manager has helped towards a more competitive game in Scotland without curbing the Scot's natural skills. I have always believed that football is a very simple game. It is only made complicated by people who basically don't understand it.

I play football simply and I believe the Scottish fans prefer it that way.

My ambitions as captain of Celtic? Well obviously I'd like nothing better than to repeat some of the successes of my predecessor Billy McNeill. He captained a Celtic team which won nine successive league titles, five Scottish Cups, and the coveted European trophy.

If I achieve any of those honours with Celtic, and further caps for my country, I hope I will always be playing the game the simple way. The way it was intended to be played.

Kenny Dalglish (below) in his part-time occupation in the motor industry.

AFTER FIVE YEARS AND COACH MOVE ON

says

★ • • • • • • • • • • • • • • • • • ★

SEPP MAIER
of
FC Bayern München
and
West Germany

★ • • • • • • • • • • • • • • • • • ★

SINCE the time that our coach Udo Lattek left Bayern München there has been a lot of rumour about problems behind the scenes. If there has been any intrigue I would surely have become aware of it, and I haven't. In fact, being the coach of Bayern is one of the easiest jobs in the football world. If we are going through a critical period, it is the sort of crisis that afflicts every top club from time to time and one that you just have to play through until things start to come right.

Sepp Maier (left) goes down to save at the feet of Johan Cruyff in the 1974 World Cup Final, and, facing page, Maier with the coveted European Cup he helped Bayern München to win.

EVERY MANAGER SHOULD

Whatever other people may say, the simple truth is that after winning everything in sight—the Bundesliga championship; the German FA Cup, the European Cup Winners Cup and the European Cup twice we were suddenly hit by a string of injuries. Other clubs are not immune to injuries of course but when you have to play without four and sometimes five of your top players for lengthy periods it is unrealistic to expect the team to go on winning in tough competition.

Uli Hoeness for example was virtually out of action for more than a year and had to undergo two operations. Then Gerd Müller had more than five months out with an injury. Such players would be missed in any team.

On a personal note about Udo Lattek, I am sure he was a very good coach but it is my opinion that after about five years with one team, every coach should change clubs.

Of course there were differing opinions about the coach—first about Udo Lattek before he left and also about our new coach Dettmar Cramer. But at every club, the manager, coach, players and fans all have different opinions. This is the way of life, in and out of football. When Bayern was winning everything, everyone, including the players was

Anyone would miss a player like Gerd Müller (above), out for five months last season says Maier, seen (facing page) giving the referee a strange look in the 1975 European Cup Final and below a shot from the only 1974 World Cup game the West Germans lost, 0–1 to East Germany—Jurgen Sparwasser (14) sprints past Horst Hottges and Berti Vogts (2).

free to speak his mind and this cannot be regarded as a problem. In my opinion it's a healthy sign as long as the players get on with the game as a team, once the discussions are over. That is how it always was at Bayern.

The key factors behind the success of Bayern, coming out of the Second Division were our chairman Mr. Wilhelm Neudecker and manager Robert Schwan. Together they built the foundations of the club in 1964 and we rose from obscurity to become the champions of Europe.

About myself and the other top goalkeepers in the Bundesliga, I know there are some critics who think that German goalkeepers are afraid of physical contact and are not good in the air. I couldn't disagree more and in my opinion German 'keepers are better than those in England!

As far as I am concerned I feel that perhaps my critics fail to appreciate my technique, maybe preferring the goalkeepers who throw themselves all

Franz Beckenbauer (above) challenges Allan Clarke—'safer than the Bank of England', says Maier.

around the penalty area. I can do that too, but that is only in emergencies. My style of play is less spectacular, based on skill in positioning and interception.

Criticism doesn't worry me. I know that had I been a poor player I couldn't have stayed ten years in the game with a top club and helped Bayern and West Germany win all the top honours. Of course I am not saying that I was always the hero but facts speak for themselves. I've played in ten Cup Finals, ranging from the World Cup; the European National championship in 1972 and two European Cup Finals . . . and never been on the losing team. I'll stand by my record.

Another myth that needs burying is the opinion I've sometimes heard about Franz Beckenbauer's style of play making his goalkeeper nervous. I've played behind Franz hundreds of times for Bayern and West Germany and am delighted to have such a player in front of me. I know he often dribbles around the penalty spot and looks to be casual at times. But it is because he is so skilled and completely in control that he has the time to look casual. In fact Beckenbauer is utterly reliable and sure of himself with the ball—he's safer than the Bank of England.

In my youth it was one of my greatest ambitions to play at Wembley and in fact, early in my career I would have jumped at the chance to play for an English club. Now however, I think the English game has many problems. I say this knowing that most English people think their national team and

their clubs are very strong and the best in Europe. Perhaps they once were—but not any more.

Now I think the English need to blend their game with the best of other European countries. The best way to do this is to engage top quality foreign players—but from the north and middle Europe—definitely not the south. In a game like football, things are always changing and it is necessary to be aware what is happening in other countries, to look and to learn.

Of course I have played against very strong English teams. At club level, Leeds and Liverpool were very strong and I liked Everton too when I saw them. But they need to add something more to their game and that I think now, can only come from other countries.

The best England team I have played against was the 1970 World Cup team when we beat them 3–2 in Mexico. This was a day when the English

Maier played for West Germany at Wembley in 1975 when England won 2–0. Below, Colin Bell celebrates the first goal which he scored with a right-foot volley.

had no luck at all and we Germans were very lucky to win. I really felt sorry for Bobby Charlton and his colleagues. It was a wonderful game and we did well to come back as we did but I could feel for the English players when they lost.

Don't misunderstand me, I say the English game has problems and perhaps I am too far away, having too little contact to really know what is wrong. But it is clear that the game in every country has problems. The English may look back and long for a new Stanley Matthews but here in Germany there are people who want to see a new young player like Beckenbauer, a new Uwe Seeler and another Gerd Müller.

We have plenty of good young players in the Bundesliga but youngsters today have other interests and broader horizons than twenty or even ten years ago. I cannot say it is wrong for young people to have other interests than football or the chance to pursue those interests but the fact is that players like Beckenbauer and Müller come along only once in thirty or forty years. They don't grow on trees.

I'm not at all pessimistic about the game as it is now, neither am I really concerned about the future. The Italians have problems, that is true, but they have had them for some years now. The English have a thriving First Division which is very competitive and the German Bundesliga runs them a very close second. The overall standard of play is higher now in the Bundesliga than it ever was.

We still have good players and contrary to what many critics think I am convinced that the top players should earn really good money. For one thing their career is short and the years of top money even shorter. And this opportunity to join the élite can only act as a spur and encourage the best young players to reach the highest standard. Surely that is the way it should be.

Maier felt sorry for Bobby Charlton and his colleagues beaten 3–2 by West Germany in the Mexico World Cup, 'the best England team I have played against', he says. In action below in his hey-day with Manchester United, Bobby Charlton beats Bryan Hamilton of Ipswich Town.

THE PRESENT CITY TEAM WILL BECOME THE BEST OF ALL

predicts
MIKE DOYLE
of
Manchester City

THE best Manchester City team I've been involved with was the side that won the FA Cup in 1969 and went on to win the European Cupwinners Cup, beating Poland's Gornik Zabrze 2–1 in the final. Having already won the championship in season 1967–68 and taken the League Cup in 1971, I have won every medal I could possibly have gained in English football plus one in Europe. But I think we played the best football around 1969–70.

That was the time when we had Joe Mercer and Malcolm Allison in charge, two men that complemented each other perfectly. Joe was a real gentleman while Malcolm was more boisterous and not very diplomatic. It was a pity they split up for

Mike Doyle demonstrates his ability in the air (photo left) and facing page another Maine Road stalwart; Joe Corrigan, collects a high ball against West Ham, two key members of the new Manchester City team being put together by manager Tony Book—photo below.

neither one has really been successful since, though I always thought Malcolm Allison would be better as a coach than he would be as a manager.

But the new team that is being created at Maine Road, given time, will I think, become even better. We've got a lot of skill, strikers who get goals regularly and we are more competitive and disciplined than the Lee, Summerbee, Bell side. Given just ordinary luck, I think Tony Book and Ian McFarlane will build a really great side.

With City I've also had medals for winning the Second Division championship and the Charity Shield and I got capped at Under 23 level and played for the Football League XI against Scotland. All I needed for a full house was the full England cap I got against Wales last march.

I'd be delighted to keep my place, but Mr. Revie has to think about the 1978 World Cup and at my age I can't expect it.

In fourteen happy years since I joined the Maine Road staff straight from school when I was 14, that championship and Cup winning team stands out in the memory. We had flair and imagination; a great willingness to work for each other and it was

Mike Summerbee (above) in his Manchester City days was 'the best forward I have known', says Mike Doyle. Photo left is of young Peter Barnes who seems certain of a bright future with City.

a joy to play. The games just couldn't come round fast enough at that time, we were so eager.

The emphasis always was on team-work but though I wouldn't say there was a key man, I think Mike Summerbee at that time was the best forward player I've known. He had good skill and was very strong and determined.

Last season we had a terrible run of injuries. Colin Bell was missing from our line up for a very long time but he was not at all the only injury we sustained. At the time it seemed like a disaster but looking back it gave Tony Book the chance to give some of our young reserves a go, and how they responded!

Peter Barnes was probably the most spectacular, but we also blooded Paul Power, Kenny Clements and Gerard Keegan who were all under 20. We have others too who will soon make their mark and with the established first team players we are soon going to have a really outstanding team.

I thought we were going to win something the previous season, the way we began the campaign. But as it turned out we were almost untouchable at home but had a wretched away record and lost out. Away from home these days you need all eleven players going at it and we just didn't have it. It's better now, for the players realised we had to do something about it. We always had the skill but we had to work harder away and match our skills with effort.

There aren't any really poor players in the First Division nowadays and as a central defender you have to treat everyone with respect and never let up for even a fraction of a second. If you do, you'll pay for it. Allan Clarke of Leeds is probably the sharpest player I've faced. He's very brave and you simply can't afford to give him even half chances.

John Radford is another player I have a very high regard for. A big strong lad, good in the air and very good at shielding the ball from you he always keeps me on my toes.

English football has taken a few knocks in recent years with England not being as successful as they should have been and gates declining. The fans generally don't like to see massed defences with forwards marked out of the game. They come to see goals.

We've never been quite so defensive in this country compared with some others who copied the Italian game and had a free back behind the defence. We play with a line of four across the back and if we've been negative it's been in midfield where some teams have played too many defensive players.

Wingers are now beginning to reappear again in many clubs and with regard to City we try to put the emphasis on getting as many midfield men forward as we can.

From what I've seen, the whole English game is in the process of change once more and I am sure we shall soon see more attacking systems. That will lead to more goals being scored and bring the crowds pouring back.

I've never been one of these pessimists who knock English football. In my opinion the British game generally has always been better than the foreigners. Our big disadvantage has been the number of competitive matches we have to play in our season.

When England games come around the players aren't physically tired but I believe they are mentally stale. Abroad, international football gets priority, with league games being cancelled before big internationals and almost every country having ten clear days to prepare for a mid-week match.

We've always had the players that were good enough but the problem is one of mental attitude and their inability to recover a sharp mental state within a few days after a heavy programme of league and cup matches.

Don Revie is clearly the most capable man we have for the England job but he faces a very difficult task indeed.

Arsenal's John Radford, in action below, 'A big strong lad, I've always had a high regard for', says Mike Doyle.

THERE ARE LOTS
NOW BUT MAY
ONE IS OU

Says MILJAN MILJANIC

◆　　◆　　◆

FOOTBALL today is going through a critical period. Nowhere is there even one outstanding team to be found—and in many countries there are lots of good players but perhaps not even one outstanding player. From the era of Ajax as a super team, FC Barcelona have Johan Cruyff and Johan Neeskens—and when they go, Barcelona will be only half a team. The Ajax super team has broken up, Bayern München are finished . . . and Juventus are nothing.

It is not a good time for watching football, but the problems are not limited to one or two countries. The problem is world wide. Even in South America, there has been a levelling down, with Peru and Colombia the finalists in the 1975 South American championship which Peru won.

When Johan Cruyff (photo left) and Johan Neeskens go, Barcelona will only be half a team, says Real Madrid boss, Miljan Miljanic, who is pictured on the right.

94

OF GOOD PLAYERS
BE NOT EVEN
STANDING

…al Madrid's Yugoslav manager

Putting the position in its simplest terms, there are not enough truly outstanding players in the game. To have a super team, it is necessary to have five or six super players and I find it difficult to count that number with the whole world to choose from, let alone in one country or one club.

Today the outstanding player must have three basic qualities above all. He must of course have a very high degree of individual skill and he must have a great knowledge of the game in terms of strategy and tactics and be very flexible in his thinking. Just as important, he must be very well prepared psychologically for in the game today there is so much pressure on the players who often have to play every three or four days for weeks on end.

Every time they play they have to be very good, under pressure from the fans and newspapers and very often television. One bad game is a catastrophe that brings increased pressure to score a resounding success in their next game.

The players today are simply being forced to play too much football.

For the top players there is league and cup football—and they are under pressure to win both.

Even players with the lowly clubs are under pressure to avoid relegation ... and quite often, to beat illustrious neighbours or the big clubs when they visit them.

When Real Madrid were at their peak they had the whole world to choose from. But no club today could do that. For one thing, many countries bar foreigners while others allow only two or three imported players. Even disregarding that however, no club in the world could afford to pay transfer fees at todays inflated prices for players like Di Stefano, Puskas, Didi, Kopa, Canario, Del Sol, even if they existed. And transfer fees are only the start. Such players command very high salaries and bonuses and no one could afford it unless they had a stadium for 250,000 people and it was sold out for every game.

In my opinion too, it would not be enough to have 11 such players today. The marking and tackling in the modern game have made it much more difficult to play and the top players need to be rested from time to time. So we must have a pool of interchangeable players and about 18 is the right number, not 11. This again adds to the costs and is another barrier to any new super team.

'When Real Madrid were at their peak, they had the whole world to choose from', writes Miljan Miljanic, 'but it would be too expensive today, and will probably never be repeated'. The team group on the right from the 1959–60 season underlines this statement, including Dominguez (goalkeeper) from Argentina, and the attack (front row from left to right) reads: Canario (Brazil), Del Sol (Spain), Di Stefano (Argentina), Puskas (Hungary) and Gento (Spain).

Miljan Miljanic (photo above) discusses a basic move in a coaching session. On the right is Gunter Netzer.

If there isn't a super team, there are perhaps twenty club sides that can be described as good; very good on their best days. Amongst these teams I would say are . . . in no particular order: Real Madrid, Borussia Mönchengladbach, FC Barcelona, Derby County, Queens Park Rangers, West Ham and Dynamo Kiev.

Some people already feel that Dynamo Kiev are on the way to being a new super team but I would be more cautious. Certainly, Dynamo do not play typical Russian football, which is very different. Dynamo come from the Ukraine where the people,

by their nature are more like Hungarians with a Latin temperament and this shows in their football. They have good skills and one or two exceptional players but I would have to see more of them against other top sides of the moment before accepting them as a new super team.

Modern defensive tactics have done much to drag the standard of play down. At first this movement was seen as a counter to super stars in attack. Centre forwards and wingers came to be marked by two men and then by degrees we saw the tight marking defensive system with a *libero* standing free, behind.

At that time it was still possible to play good football and open the defence if you had outstanding midfield players who could control the central areas and move forward often—with the ball and without

98

it—to become extra forwards. Such players could set centre forwards free by dribbling at the men marking them; they could go right through a defence with the ball and take on the *libero*. But in time, the defence came to take the midfield within its scope and tight marking was introduced there too so·that we find today that seven or eight players, even nine in some cases, are played as defenders whose duty it is to control their immediate opponent.

In spite of the super-defence I am optimistic about the future of the game.

This is primarily because no one can hope to mark every player; double mark stars ... and still have a free man behind the defence.

The key men now in many ways are those whom many people call the back four, and in particular, the full backs. Many teams have tried to use their full backs as attacking players but most have been only moderately successful because they have tried to take advantage of their relative freedom by asking full backs to move upfield. What we must do is develop a new generation of full backs, if necessary converting young inside forwards!

It is foolish to expect a regular full back to move

'There is no "super-team" today', says Miljanic, 'but amongst the good sides are Derby County' whose best player is surely Colin Todd (in action left) 'and Dynamo Kiev' whose explosive centre forward Vladimir Onitchenko is pictured below.

upfield and dribble past good defenders, think like generals and finish their moves with telling passes. This is where most 'attacking backs' fall down for though it is relatively easy to move upfield and get the ball, it is the quality of their final pass that counts.

Natural full backs cannot be converted apart from the very rare exception. A new generation of the new style will have to be developed. Of course there are exceptions to this. Paul Breitner who joined us from Bayern München is the best one but he is almost unique. Always looking, always thinking, quite quick and a good dribbler with lots of stamina. But I think he was wasted at left back.

In my opinion he was always a natural midfield player and when he came to Real Madrid he swapped his number 3 shirt for number 8 and settled into his new role without any trouble at all.

It was a wrench for me to join Real Madrid for I had behind me 28 unbroken years with Red Star, Belgrade. First I had ten years playing at left half in the first team and when I retired I began coaching some of the juniors. My family were all with Red Star—my wife played handball for the club and even now my 17 years old son plays football for one of their youth teams.

Tight-marking today is really tight, see photo left from the 1974 World Cup Final, Berti Vogts glued to Johan Cruyff even when he doesn't have the ball. German left back, Paul Breitner, (portrait above) and shooting at the Real Sociedad goal (facing page) is unique says Miljanic.

Yugoslavia has always produced good players and Red Star have often been the backbone of the national team. Very largely this is due to their very serious approach to the game and the care they take in developing young players. They have for example three teams for players between 10 and 12 years—and so on up to 18. All told there are 13 junior teams looked after by 6 full time coaches!

I took the Real Madrid job largely because it was a great honour remembering the club's past exploits and reputation. But it would be wrong if I did not also admit that I am also being very well paid and under Spanish tax laws I keep the greater part of my earnings. But money isn't everything and being part of a very happy club I feel I must pay tribute to the Real Chairman, Don Santiago Bernabeu.

Don Santiago is of course a very astute business man, but in my experience he is also unique among club chairmen in that he is also a very fine sportsman.

"THE BEST CONT[INENTALS] SCORE IN TIGH[T] THAN US"

NENTALS CAN
TER SITUATIONS

THE ambition of every footballer must be to play for his country, and I am no exception. I have enjoyed every game I've had with England so far and my only regret is that I haven't been involved with a successful team that has been able to win matches consistently.

Trevor Brooking (portrait right) and after putting away a vital goal for West Ham against Spurs (left) watched by Pat Jennings and Don McAllister says 'English players need more space in which to shoot, and are not so accurate as the best foreigners in their finishing.'

We have plenty of talented players available for England, but as I see it, the same set of players don't stay together long enough to develop the kind of understanding that we see at club level. New caps, and those who, like me, have only had a few games, often fail to reproduce their club form because they are too cautious. Trying to play well, they tend to play safe and keep things simple instead of playing their natural game.

Only if the side gets a good result in your first game do you feel confident about keeping your place but even then it may be some months before the next England game. So the understanding that is vital takes quite a while to develop.

It's something of a vicious circle. Unless the same team, more or less, gets a good few games together they can't develop into a good side. Understanding

Billy Bonds (photo right) was badly missed last season while out of the game for a long time with a thigh injury and below, Alan Taylor goes up for a high cross, which, says Brooking, English players resort to, too often.

and good team-work only come with familiarity and the confidence to play your natural game— which is what you have been selected for based on your club form. It only starts to develop after a run of games that helps build up your confidence. But, and here's the rub, if England don't get good results consistently, then the manager comes under pressure to change the team.

But there is another factor when we meet top class continental opposition that I think is critical. This is our comparative inability to accept scoring chances, and it all comes down to the continentals being superior in this department.

Facing page (above) Reipas Lahti goalkeeper Harri Holli goes down to save at the feet of West Ham's Alan Taylor and Billy Jennings (9), and below, Mervyn Day dives at full stretch to cut out a cross meant for Tottenham's John Duncan, with Mick McGiven close by.

In league football, English players frequently face massed defences and tend to resort too often to the hopeful high cross. We put the ball up into the goalmouth, virtually saying to our strikers 'go on, fight for that and score'. On the continent, the best teams and therefore the best players are more skilful in their approach to goal and in their finishing. They try to play the ball into the penalty area to feet—and their strikers have the necessary skills to shield the ball from opponents, making it difficult to challenge, and the ability to get in accurate shots in tight situations. English players generally need more space in which to shoot and are not so accurate in their finishing.

At West Ham we work every week on turning, screening the ball and hitting shots in tight situations but unfortunately many clubs do not yet do it. For some reason they go on looking to the high cross for their goals. The result is that every week in league and cup games I see in matches I play in

The man for man marking of the Italians clearly illustrated in this shot (above) from the England–Italy game in November, 1973. Colin Bell, left, and Peter Osgood are both closely marked and England lost 1–0 after having most of the play.

and in the televised games I watch, chances, or half chances, being missed by English players that the top continentals would often score from.

It has I think been this lack of ability in finishing which led to Poland drawing 1–1 at Wembley; West Germany beating England 3–1 at Wembley and England being held to home and away draws by Portugal. All these results have led to England's elimination from two consecutive European championships and the 1974 World Cup. Even the Czechs when we played them in Bratislava were better in their finishing.

For the 1978 World Cup the Italians are clearly going to be the major rivals and in my experience, any Italian side is difficult to break down because they are so defensive. Clearly they play the most defensive football of all with every player tight marked man for man. Being marked by an opponent who doesn't watch the ball but only watches the man he is marking is an unusual experience that we don't get in England.

When you can't break down an Italian defence the players tend to get frustrated and unless you are very careful, they suddenly break out, sneak a goal to lead 1–0 and you get more frustrated than ever. Against Italy, in both matches, England will have to maintain 100% concentration throughout the 90 minutes and not allow themselves to become frustrated. You just have to be patient, keep plugging away and take the chances when they come.

Luxembourg shouldn't be a problem but I have a high regard for the Finns who have improved a great deal. They held Italy to a 0–0 draw in Rome last season and for West Ham in the European Cupwinners Cup we were held to 2–2 away to their Cup winners Reipas Lahti. Finland could swing this group by sneaking a point from either England or Italy and it will be up to the England players to make sure it doesn't happen to them by being aware that the Finns have improved and not taking the games too easily.

I have a particular interest in playing against Finland for my wife Hilkka comes from there. We met some time ago when I went with West Ham to play a friendly match in Helsinki against one of their leading clubs, HJK who were celebrating their 50th anniversary that year. I've been back there several times since then for holidays. It's a very picturesque country full of lakes and forests but I'm sure that the England game in Helsinki will be no picnic, as it probably would have been a few years ago.

Though the Finns are near amateur even they have improved their skills, which brings me back to an earlier theme. I think the plain fact is that the continental players are more skilful on the ball— and perhaps a bit more lazy. Our game at club level is geared more to physical things, running and stamina and I think we've lost out a bit in recent years in terms of ball skills.

What certainly doesn't help is the tendency for youngsters in school teams to be forced to copy the 4–3–3 system most league clubs use. At that level also, the emphasis now seems to be on running and

Frank Lampard (above) who has been playing consistently well, and West Ham fans wonder why he hasn't been awarded more England caps.

work rate rather than skill and I just can't see a new Stan Matthews or Tommy Finney coming through the system we have at schoolboy level.

My biggest failing, which I recognise, is that I like the ball too much. If I wasn't a professional I would be playing as an amateur every Saturday and Sunday just for pleasure, but I don't enjoy the hard running that is necessary to play at top level. Training with the ball, working at skills and shooting practice I could do all day, but I'm not a naturally good runner. Billy Bonds my West Ham clubmate is a natural. He could miss training for a week or two and come back from injury straight into the first team and do well, chasing about with all his

Tottenham's midfield schemer Steve Perryman who Trevor Brooking has a high regard for. They usually mark each other in club games.

natural energy and enthusiasm.

Most people seem to agree that my failing is a lack of consistency in my game. I know it and I think I know why and have worked at it for the last two years or so. I lack aggression which is something I'm sure I have improved on, but I have to exercise strict mental discipline in training.

Sometimes I find that I have to keep jerking myself into action while in other games I just click straight away. I think I have to train hard, physically, to play well but I'm sure I have improved in this. I have to train hard to stay sharp and maybe also I fall down in pace over the first yard or two, but that again is something I have worked on.

At club level you develop an understanding with your colleagues by playing and training together regularly. For this reason many people have come to the view that to concentrate England's choice from three or perhaps four clubs would help.

West Ham have several other players who could make it at international level and that for example would help me play better for England. Billy Bonds could have made it I think, but he had a niggling groin injury for more than a year that pegged him back. Frank Lampard too has been playing consistently well for a long time and Kevin Lock is a young player with a bright future.

Clearly though, the longer periods that England are going to have together before matches will be a big help. I remember the morning of the 1–1 draw with Portugal in Lisbon when we had four players who had to have fitness tests just hours before the match. Playing competitive football only four days before a vital international is no way to prepare. It would also help England if we had fewer league and cup games in England, as they do on the continent, but that's something that I cannot see coming.

Being a natural attacking player I'm not too keen on defensive duties and marking opponents, but at international level it has increasingly become 11 against 11 and you can't afford not to be involved with marking. This is another aspect of my game that I have worked on.

Even in club games I find that as an attacking player I am tight marked, usually by players who can break forward themselves so I have to get involved. Steve Perryman is one player I have a high regard for and when we play Spurs we usually mark each other and have had many rare tussles. He is quick and sharp and very useful on the ball too.

Brian Talbot of Ipswich is another difficult player to play against who does his best to stifle me. He is very sharp in the tackle and has apparently endless energy. The trick is to find space in which to receive the ball and deny space to your opponents when they have the ball. International football is like that now, and the more defensive the game gets the more difficult it becomes to find space and use your skill. This is where we fall down internationally, not being able to use our skill in tight situations, but we must work on it and I am sure we will.

NEWCASTLE UNITED HAVE THE PLAYERS AND THE SUPPORT, BUT . . .

by
STEWART BARROWCLOUGH

ONE of the most baffling mysteries in football must be the inability of Newcastle United to win something big. We've got the players, in my time we've always had plenty of good players and with our support we should be one of the leading clubs in the country, but somehow something always seems to go wrong.

On our day we have beaten all the top teams, even Liverpool and Leeds United but then we seem to follow that by losing to clubs like Wolverhampton Wanderers and Burnley when they are having a bad time.

Personally, I had two very good seasons I think, between 1972 and 1974 but all I have to show for it in the way of medals is one from the Anglo-Italian Cup which we won in 1973.

I haven't done badly for a boy from Barnsley where I played Fourth Division football. Newcastle bought me for a £55,000 fee which is still the highest fee Barnsley have ever received. But like Newcastle I seem to go so far and then something goes wrong.

That's how it was when we reached the FA Cup Final in 1974 only to lose at Wembley, 3–0 against Liverpool. I hardly missed a game that season, played in every round of the Cup up to the semi-final and missed that game because I had 'flu. Then manager Joe Harvey decided to keep the winning team from the semi-final and all I could do was watch the lads go down to Liverpool.

Mr. Harvey was big enough to admit he might have made a mistake not playing me which was a bit of a consolation. After the game he told me 'I wish I had played you now. Our strikers hardly got a kick of the ball and if you had been on the wing and had a good game we might have won.'

After that Cup Final when Newcastle seemed to dry up it wasn't really a surprise that Joe Harvey was replaced. He is still with the club as a scout but instead of building on that relative success in the FA Cup, the following season we went out of the Football League Cup to Chester and Walsall beat

Stewart Barrowclough (photo left) in full cry. 'Malcolm Macdonald is only a shade faster than me', he says, 'perhaps one yard in a hundred.'

'Supermac', Malcolm Macdonald (photo right) with one eye on the middle and his deadly left foot poised.

us in the FA Cup. We'd already been there—knocked out of the FA Cup by Hereford in 1972 when they were a non-League club.

Joe was a great bloke, popular with all the players but I suppose he lacked what most successful managers have in that he didn't have the touch of luck when he needed it. Anyway the Directors obviously decided it was time to change manager and appointed Gordon Lee at the start of last season.

Mr. Lee had already proved himself by taking Blackburn Rovers up into the Second Division as Division III champions but his coming has brought me a lean spell.

As a winger you might think I would have suffered in the years when Sir Alf Ramsey won the World Cup without wingers and almost everyone copied his system. But I always kept my place on the wing—and Alf even gave me Under 23 caps as an orthodox winger.

But Mr. Lee thinks that playing me on the right wing would be a luxury he cannot afford because then our midfield would not be strong enough. I'm not suggesting that he's wrong but it's a bit frustrating being substitute almost every week.

Even when I have been in the side I have been asked to work in midfield—though I'm still allowed to make occasional breaks down the wing too. But I'm not really a midfield player. The boss told me very soon after he arrived how he was intending to play but assured me that he would do everything possible to strengthen the midfield and having done that, then I would get a run in the side. But clubs with good midfield players are double eager to keep them and the kind of player Mr. Lee requires doesn't become available for transfer very often. So I had to wait, trying to be patient until he could buy the man he needs.

Perhaps if I scored more goals it might all be different. I get a few but I'm not what you'd call a frequent scorer and to be honest I'm not very good in the air. Speed is my biggest asset, that and the ability to take people on which makes me an ideal

type to play on the wing. Maybe my pace doesn't show as it does with Malcolm Macdonald but though I've never timed myself over 100 yards, Malcolm is just a shade faster than me, perhaps he'd beat me by a yard in a hundred.

Still, I've been lucky to have had the chance to make my living from playing football. Certainly I've visited many parts of the world that I could never have afforded to visit as a tourist on holiday. Hong Kong and Bangkok are probably the two most fantastic places I've been to. Though if I had to choose another country, apart from England in which to live, I think it would be Switzerland or Norway. I like mountain scenery and clear, clean air.

Playing in Bangkok was a real experience. The players were all very small and their standard of

Goalkeeper Mike Mahoney (photo above) beaten here by a header from Tottenham's John Pratt, and striker Alan Gowling (facing page) seen in a tussle with Ipswich Town's Mick Mills, were two of the key figures in Newcastle's Cup campaigns last season.

play was probably non-league by comparison with the game in England but they had a lovely stadium. And thousands turned up to see the locals play Newcastle on a glorious evening.

I've heard it said that English fans wouldn't turn up every week to see the kind of football the top class continentals play. That might be true in London and maybe other parts of the country but I'm sure it's not true in the North East.

Photo (left) Pele, the most incredible player Barrowclough has ever seen. Below, Don Masson who has tremendous skills, and right, a portrait of Willie Donachie, the best left back Barrowclough has played against.

Last season Newcastle had a good run, getting consistently good results but winning 1–0 or 2–1. Week after week the local papers were full of letters from readers saying they think Newcastle should play better football. I may be wrong but I find myself in sympathy with the Newcastle fans for I like teams like Holland as they were in the 1974 World Cup particularly with all their defenders really skilful.

Amongst other English teams, I like watching Queens Park Rangers who have Stan Bowles, Gerry Francis and Don Masson. I saw Masson three times last season and he's so skilful he never seems to lose the ball!

Of course the best of the continentals are really fantastic. Players like Cruyff and Müller are idolised everywhere but the most incredible player I ever saw was Pelé. I played against him in a friendly match between Newcastle and Santos in Hong Kong. We were 2–1 up at half time but lost 4–2 at the end with Pelé scoring a hat trick. One of his goals was really out of this world.

Pelé was being marked by Bobby Moncur but on one occasion he was left a mere spectator. Pelé received the ball on his head, dropped it down to his thigh, flicked it with his knee, dropped the ball onto his foot and volleyed a great shot!

Over the years Newcastle fans have seen some great players—though they'll never have one as good as Pelé—and this I think is what our fans are restive about. They are accustomed to watching good football and they want to see a good game as well as a good result for the club.

For myself I've always enjoyed my football and I have fond memories of many a keen battle with a good left back. Manchester City's Willie Donachie is probably the best back I've faced. He's got everything, quick, strong and very skilful. Another fine player I played against at Under 23 level is Celtic's Danny McGrain who is now a regular choice for Scotland. I'd love to meet him again in an England–Scotland match.

IF A YOUNGSTER SHOWS TALENT, HIS FATHER THE MONEY TO

THINKS OF
BE MADE

writes
WIM VAN HANEGEM
inside left of
FEYENOORD
and
HOLLAND

Wim Van Hanegem (above right) says Holland threw away the 1974 World Cup Final because some of the players 'tried to humiliate the Germans'. Photo left shows two of Van Hanegem's Feyenoord colleagues Joop Van Daele and Austrian striker Willy Kreuz (centre) in action against Kevin Beattie of Ipswich last season.

FEYENOORD failed to win either the Cup or the League in 1974–75 and we got off to a bad start in last seasons programme but we improved and I am sure we will come again. The problems we had were only of a temporary nature. Principally, some of the players lacked the right approach to the game in the new situation with a new, strange manager and on top of that we had an awful lot of injuries.

To have a good successful team today you need at least 18 players, all equally talented. Having transferred Peter Ressel to Anderlecht and Lex Schoenmaeker who were both fast and talented strikers to a Dutch club, we were short of goal-scoring power. In the middle of the season we signed Nico Jansen from FC Amsterdam—a very good centre forward—and I am sure he will make a difference in the long run.

117

For myself, although I am now 31 and the oldest player in the team I am still fit and well and I believe, well able to do my part. As a matter of fact I had a very good start to last season but then got a nasty injury to an achilles tendon. Fit again, I was suspended for several weeks by the Dutch FA and neither event helped the team very much.

One of the critical points was the arrival of our new manager from Poland Mr. Brzezanczyk. He couldn't speak Dutch and none of the players liked him at first. He seemed to have quite different ideas about football and couldn't make us believe in him. It was a clear case of lack of communication.

When it became clear that things weren't going to work it was decided to get together and talk things out. One of the biggest differences of opinion was that he thought Wim Jansen should play an

Dutch captain Johan Cruyff (photo above) and his Polish counterpart Kazimierz Deyna, shake hands before Poland's 4–1 win in Chorzow last autumn. On the right, from the same match Wim Van Hanegem on the ball in his usual crouching style with Johan Neeskens (6) looking on.

attacking game in midfield while I played defensively. The whole team disagreed and we had a hard time convincing him. Finally he agreed to give it a chance playing our way and from then on the team played much better. After that the understanding between the manager and the players was as good as possible between Dutch players and a Polish manager.

Many outsiders were surprised when it was decided in the summer of 1975 not to renew the contract of our manager Wiel Coerver. Without trying to belittle him or his work, I must say that in his time, Feyenoord were quite the best team in Holland. Never in my nine years with the club have we won the championship so easily. But in the end Coerver went the wrong way through talking too much and in different ways to different players. For example he told Boskamp how he should play to push one of the regulars out of the team and take his place . . . and such things set people by the ears.

In that way he lost his grip on the team completely and when his contract expired there was no reason to keep him. A manager has to do more than look after the physical condition of the players—his most important task I think is to keep the spirit of the team alive, and that is where he failed.

Despite Holland's World Cup success and the European Cup victories of Ajax and Feyenoord it is not so long ago that we were just amateurs. In fact I can remember those times myself.

As a teenager I lived in Utrecht and my only interest was playing football, in the streets and on a recreation ground in my neighbourhood. One day I went to the training ground of Velox, watching from behind the goal while a coach worked with a goalkeeper. Quite often the shots went wide and I returned the ball for them. It must suddenly have struck the coach that I was rather skilled because he stopped the training and came and asked me if I was signed by any club. I was 16 then and said no.

He asked me to sign for Velox and the next Sunday I played in their senior youth team and three months later I was a part-time professional.

Five years later I was transferred to Xerxes of Rotterdam where I stayed for two years and then became a full professional with Feyenoord. This was just at the time when the game in Holland was beginning to reach a climax.

The secret of the rise in Dutch football? I don't believe there was one. We changed from amateurism, training twice a week after work, in the evenings if the weather wasn't too bad—and giving it a miss if we didn't fancy it—to professionalism, busy with

Feyenoord World Cup midfield player Wim Jansen (above) and photo right, Jan Everse beats Trevor Whymark to the ball in an UEFA Cup game.

football all day. Furthermore, I don't think that the game in Holland is stronger than anywhere else. West Germany, England, Italy and Spain for example are equally strong.

Somehow a story seems to have got about that I have often refused to play for Holland in international matches. I do remember that before I joined Feyenoord some of their players did, but I have never done so. In March, 1975 I did tell the Dutch FA, the KNVB, that I *would* refuse to play if the referees and the Disciplinary Committee did not stop trying to make me a black sheep.

At that time I wasn't allowed to move an inch without being penalised and I really felt that I was being hunted. The way I was being treated, suspensions and fines that robbed me of almost half the bonuses the FA paid me for playing in the 1974 World Cup made me very bitter. Finally, a searching talk with one of the top FA officials cleared the air and I gave in.

Neither have there been any rivalries between Feyenoord and Ajax players in the Dutch squad. There was some trouble between players of PSV Eindhoven and the rest of the squad in 1975 but I wasn't there so I cannot really comment.

As far as I am concerned I just like playing football. I feel the same playing for Holland as I do for my club . . . and I'm sure I will play for a local team and enjoy it just as much when my professional career is over.

One big problem in Holland and I suppose every other country is that youngsters today don't practice as much as my generation did. Not long ago I went for a trip to Utrecht and visited the neighbourhood where my family lived when I was young. In my time the streets were empty and there were practically no cars. Now they stood bumper to bumper on both sides of the street and there was no place left to kick a ball around.

When I was 13–14–15 I was playing football all day long but most youngsters today seem to spend more time at a disco than they do playing football. And if a youngster does show signs of skill, his father is only interested in the money that might be made out of football. I really don't know where this general attitude will lead to and I don't see any remedy either!

Here in Holland lots of people don't like Johan Cruyff any more. They say: 'he doesn't talk about football now, only money'. In the end this becomes very boring indeed. I need money too as everyone does and it's very convenient if one can spend what one likes. But that doesn't mean there's nothing else in the world, and Johan often seems to act as if money is the most important thing, indeed the only thing.

Having said that I think Cruyff is still one of the best players the world has ever known. He and I have always been good friends since we first met at Zeist where the Dutch national team train, and playing together things couldn't be better.

It's different of course when we play in opposite teams, then he becomes just another player. His football is still outstanding but I think he now plays in a different way. I sometimes think he starts thinking about money while he's playing, but once in a while he still shows how skilful he is.

I had heard such a lot about the Ajax manager Rinus Michels that I was really eager to find out if everything the Ajax players told me about him was true.

The World Cup gave me the opportunity, for before that we had never met but I was more than a little anxious about it when the time came. Michels arrived from Spain to take over the Dutch squad and decided that next day he would see all the players individually according to our numbers. My number was 7 but I asked Wim Jansen (who was 8) to go in before me and I went off to play tennis. Thus when I went in to face Michels I was still in my tennis outfit when I entered the office.

'Been playing tennis?' Michels asked me.

'Yes' I replied.

'Going to play tennis again after we've finished talking?' asked Michels.

I thought for a minute and then said yes, and Michels replied . . . 'O.K. you can go'.

I couldn't believe it for he'd been closetted with each of the other players for about an hour or more.

Michels must have seen the disbelief in my eyes for he then went on 'What is there I can tell you about football? I know your skill and how you play. You play just as you usually do and I'm sure everything will work out all right.'

Usually I am never one to be short of words but on that occasion I was both surprised and speechless. As I left him, I felt that he had burdened me with a tremendous responsibility. One that I had never known before.

What a way to motivate a player!

It was of course a big disappointment that we were beaten in the World Cup final but certainly it was not the managers fault. The responsibility rests solely with some of the players.

First of all, Holland has never been very fond (politically) of the Germans. Then during the World Cup we had been sickened by the stories in the German papers and comments on TV about how lucky we had been, and how they would beat us . . . and so on. Then suddenly we were 1–0 up, and some of the players—I was among them—had only one wish: to humiliate the Germans, to ridicule them.

Only half the team tried to play as planned and when the Germans made a comeback we fell apart and were simply unable to regain a grip on the game.

ASTON VILLA'S RAY GRAYDON

says

'I AM FORTUNATE TO BE WITH A GREAT CLUB'

ALTHOUGH some team managers still seem disinclined to play with wingers my feeling is that to be really successful in the top class game today you must have at least one genuine winger and preferably two. This opinion seems to be endorsed by the successful teams on the continent which was probably sparked off by the fact that the finalists in the 1974 World Cup, West Germany and Holland, both fielded two wingers.

Here in England many teams are still playing to a 4–4–2 formation which usually includes what you might call part-time wingers. They line up in midfield and break out wide from there down the flanks, but they are withdrawn into midfield to do their share of the running and working.

I have mastered this part of my game in the last few seasons, playing on the right in midfield and when the opportunity arose, breaking away down the wing. But to me, the success last season of Manchester United who had two genuine wingers in Coppell and Hill, really points the way to the future.

A recent portrait of Graydon . . . right.

123

The biggest influence on me was not one of the managers or coaches of clubs I've played for but my father. He wasn't a professional but he played as an amateur, and everyone I've spoken to who saw him play, tells me he was a good player. He aroused my interest in the game as a baby and I owe him a great deal. Even now my mother and father make the trek from Bristol to Birmingham to see all my games for Aston Villa.

Flashback to Ray Graydon's big day when his goal took the Football League Cup to Villa Park in 1975. Below, Norwich 'keeper Kevin Keelan punches clear amongst a mass of Villa players. Facing page (below), Chris Nicholl and Ian Ross parade the Trophy at the end, and above left, Graydon salutes the Villa fans at the final whistle.

At school I began as a defender and moved by stages to the wing. A right back at first, I was switched first to wing half as it was in those days and later to inside forward, but before I left school I was regularly playing on the wing.

Bristol Rovers signed me as an apprentice professional but after twelve months I decided I needed a career outside the game to give me a secure future. I served a four year apprenticeship, qualifying as an electrician. At this time I was capped for England Amateur Youth and then began playing for Bristol Rovers as a part-time professional.

Somehow I just didn't enjoy playing for Rovers as an apprentice and left to play for an amateur club called Hambrook in the Bristol Premier Combination. Then Bert Tann, Rovers' manager at the time promised me a run of six games in the Reserves at the end of the season. I signed as a full professional at twenty-one under Fred Ford and he was followed

125

by Bill Dodgin Senior who arranged my transfer to Aston Villa. Rovers received £25,000 and the Villa captain Brian Godfrey in part exchange, and I moved to Birmingham.

I had scored 33 goals for Bristol Rovers and I chipped in my share for Villa in that first season which was one of the most satisfying seasons I've had to date, for we won promotion as Third Division champions under manager Vic Crowe with a record 70 points.

Helping Villa win the League Cup was my fondest memory but I still think that first promotion year was very satisfying.

Of course the 1974–75 season was a real success, promotion to Division I and a League Cup Winners medal is no mean achievement. The Wembly Cup Final is really more of an occasion than a game and though the critics didn't think much of our 1–0 win over Norwich City, I'd like to play there in a final every year, good games or not.

Amongst all the goals I've scored the one I got at Wembley was the one that stands out in my memory; not because it was a good goal, but because it was so important. For the benefit of those that might have forgotten it came from a penalty which Norwich 'keeper Kevin Keelan half saved and pushed against a post. I got the rebound, controlled the ball and scored . . . and the League Cup went to Villa Park.

That promotion and League Cup double created a lot of excitement amongst the Villa fans but I really think they deserved it. Villa have always had a great following, even in the years of their slide to

Bobby McDonald (white shirt, below) was one of Villa's successes last season, and facing page, Ray Graydon away on the wing.

the Third Division and it was great to be in the side that brought them some tangible reward and put them back in the First Division.

1974–75 didn't start like a successful year for we struggled quite a bit before Christmas. The turning point came in a Cup game against Oldham that gave us our first away win and that seemed to boost everyone's morale and set us off on a good run. We had some tough games and I remember particularly a very dour 0–0 draw away to Sunderland and of course that narrow Wembley win, but all round effort and team spirit saw us through.

We had a hard time settling down in the First Division particularly away from home, but we badly missed our two strikers Brian Little and Keith Leonard, who is one of our most consistent scorers. They missed most of last season because of cartilage operations. In the First Division it's very difficult to pick up points away from home and though we experimented with different playing formations, trying to find the right formula, I don't suppose it will ever be easy.

Given time I think we can do well for we have a very good set of players. Chris Nicholl of course is a current international for Northern Ireland and goalkeeper John Burridge settled down very well

after he joined us from Blackpool, but I could go on right through the side for our game is based on all round effort and individual skills harnessed within the team framework.

Though Derby County have taken honours to the Midlands, the Birmingham–West Brom–Wolverhampton area has not seen too much success in recent years but I am sure these things go in cycles. Some teams are lucky enough to find good players and get good managers while others perhaps need only one or two players to become good teams. But Villa's turn will come soon I think.

Whatever success we might have at Villa Park I really believe the club and their followers deserve it. I was always aware of their great traditions and their big following and that was why I was so pleased to sign for them. I consider myself extremely fortunate to be associated with a great club.

Goalkeeper John Burridge (in action below) settled down very well with us, writes Ray Graydon. Facing page, what better way to complete a book than with an action shot of 'Der Kaiser', the incomparable Franz Beckenbauer.

THE YEAR'S FOOTBALL

THE 1978 World Cup looms ahead but 1975 was essentially the year of the Europeans seeking places in the last eight of the European Football Championship. Those national football associations, like England and Scotland, who failed to qualify can seek to console themselves with brave words about preparing for the World Cup qualifying campaigns but the honours of the year must go to the eight FAs who did qualify for the European quarter-finals. And, so far as Britain was concerned, that meant only Wales.

England had started well with a convincing 3–0 victory at Wembley against Czechoslovakia in October 1974 but then made things difficult by only drawing at home against Portugal three weeks later. In January 1973 England had similarly dropped a home point against Wales in the qualifying competition for the 1974 World Cup and, in these small qualifying groups, it is the points surrendered at home that foreshadow ultimate failure and, conversely of course, the points gained away that point towards success.

The complete results in the qualifying competition for the European Football Championship (reproduced on the following pages) are worth considering. In England's Group One, Czechoslovakia, England and Portugal all took the maximum four points from the minnow in the group, Cyprus, but Czechoslovakia won all three of their home matches, England dropped one point at home and Portugal two, and those dropped points determined the final positions.

In Groups 2 and 3, the final group leaders, Wales and Yugoslavia respectively, were in each group the only country with one hundred per cent home points. Group Four, won by Spain with Scotland in third place, with the same number of points as second-placed Rumania but with a poorer goal-difference, was a curious one bristling with drawn matches, but again it was Scotland's home defeat against Spain in the Scots first match that ultimately decided the issue with both Spain and Rumania undefeated at home. Rumania spoiled their chances

by only drawing away to both Denmark and Scotland where Spain had each time won. Rumania's 1975 record was a remarkable one with nine of the ten matches played drawn—six of them one-all and three two-all!

In Groups 5 and 6, again the group leaders, the Netherlands and the Soviet Union, were three times home winners. In Group 6 so too were the Republic of Ireland and their brave failure was only because whereas the Soviet Union gained two away points from a win against Switzerland, the Irish had to be content with one from their drawn match in Turkey. It was nonetheless a fine effort by a side picked from so small a field of professional players.

Group 7 was notable for the refusal of the minnow in the group, Iceland, to be the chopping block for Belgium, East Germany and France. East Germany one feels really should have won the group but they had started badly in the three matches played in 1974 with a *home* point dropped against Iceland partly off-set with a draw in Paris against France but then aggravated by another point conceded at home against Belgium. And worse was to follow in June 1975 when the East Germans were beaten in Reykjavik by Iceland by the odd goal in three. The East Germans then tried to pick themselves up and finished their group matches with an away win against Belgium and a home win against France. Belgium however had safely collected five out of a possible six points from their three matches played in 1974 (compared with the East Germans three out of six) and a home win against Iceland and a draw away to France saw the Belgians safely home at the top. Three out of four points lost to Iceland was too much leeway for the East Germans but Iceland gained one further point from a home draw against France. With all due regard to Wales' fine overall showing—including that splendid win over the Hungarians in Budapest, I think if I had to award an individual honour for 1975 it would be to Iceland. And that means to Tony Knapp who has done such a remarkable coaching job for the

Icelanders. As I write the bitter 'cod war' between Iceland and Britain seems likely to have jeopardised the return of Tony Knapp to Iceland to carry on his work there. One hopes that he has been able to return so that the future development of football in Iceland can be noted.

Also, as I write, Group 8 is not completed with West Germany, the reigning world champions, due to play a final match at home against Malta and needing only to draw that match to finish one point ahead of Greece. Curiously Greece, despite good performances in drawing away to both West Germany and Bulgaria, were beaten away to Malta where, as expected, West Germany and Bulgaria were successful. That West Germany have had to rely upon the outcome of their final match is an indication of the fact that they have not been particularly impressive in the qualifying matches. The West Germans suffer, as do England and to a lesser extent Scotland but definitely not Wales and Northern Ireland, from having too many players of at or around *international* class from whom to select their team. Given three or four *world class* players — Banks, Moore, Bobby Charlton for examples for England in 1966, Vogts, Beckenbauer, Overath, Gerd Müller for example for West Germany in 1974, it is usually possible to permutate the remaining seven or eight from say sixteen to twenty other players and still have a very good national side. Without those world class players, or with declining world class players, ringing the changes in the hope of stumbling on the right blend can result in less successful national sides than the more settled ones of countries like Wales and the two Irelands.

There is substance of course in the complaints of Don Revie (and of Alf Ramsey before him) that he does not get enough pre-match time to properly prepare the national team he has selected, and that may be less of a handicap to Wales who, with far fewer to select from, more often field a settled side.

During 1975 no fewer than 25 different players wore the England shirt in the nine matches played. Colin Todd was the only one hundred per cent ever-present; Dave Watson and Mike Channon, including substitutions, also appeared in every match played; Ray Clemence missed only the home match against Cyprus (which match did not really give Peter Shilton much international practice in goal!) but in midfield there seemed to be more hope than conviction in the selections of such as Hudson and Viljoen (twice apiece) and Currie and Brooking (once each).

Scotland, with probably fewer international class players to select from, even allowing for the inclusion of English-born players like Harvey and Rioch, were even more unsettled than England. In their 10 matches played in 1975, 38 different players made their appearances whether regularly like Dalglish or briefly like Burns and Souness.

Wales, by comparison, used 18 players in their six matches and Northern Ireland the same number in seven matches and such changes as those countries made were generally enforced ones because of injury or non-availability.

The historical separate existence of the four British national FAs in a single country, with its hundreds of years of free movement so far as place of livelihood and residence is concerned, obviously produces a situation in which English football clubs, no less than English factories, offices, shops, schools and so on, have staffs made up of the 'four' nations, and the theory of a national team based around a single successful club has seldom been practicable in England. The Soviet Union, another country with a very large pool of potential national team players, have put the theory into practice with their full national team based on the very fine Dynamo Kiev side that so delightfully won the 1975 European Cup Winners Cup, and their Olympic side (in effect their 'B' team) based on the players of Moscow Torpedo.

Mention of the Olympics reminds me that 1975 saw the qualifying matches played for the 1976 Games in Montreal. The status of these matches is always debatable. The simple rule I have applied in considering the matches is that where such a match is between two national sides selected from all each country's players that can fairly be regarded as a Full international match. In the Austria, Czechoslovakia, East Germany group for example, the last two named could pick their strongest teams whereas Austria had to exclude acknowledged professional players. Matches involving Austria could not be regarded as Full internationals therefore but those between such as East Germany and Czechoslovakia can be.

GORDON JEFFERY

EUROPEAN FOOTBALL CHAMPIONSHIP 1976

Qualifying Competition

Group I

Home Team	Cz.	Eng.	Por.	Cyp.	P	W	D	L	F	A	Pts
CZECHOSLOVAKIA	–	2–1	5–0	4–0	6	4	1	1	15	5	9
England	3–0	–	0–0	5–0	6	3	2	1	11	3	8
Portugal	1–1	1–1	–	1–0	6	2	3	1	5	7	7
Cyprus	0–3	0–1	0–2	–	6	0	0	6	0	16	0

Group II

	Wal.	Hung.	Aus.	Lux.	P	W	D	L	F	A	Pts
WALES	–	2–0	1–0	5–0	6	5	0	1	14	4	10
Hungary	1–2	–	2–1	8–1	6	3	1	2	15	8	7
Austria	2–1	0–0	–	6–2	6	3	1	2	11	7	7
Luxembourg	1–3	2–4	1–2	–	6	0	0	6	7	28	0

Group III

	Yug.	N.I.	Swe.	Nor.	P	W	D	L	F	A	Pts
YUGOSLAVIA	–	1–0	3–0	3–1	6	5	0	1	12	4	10
N. Ireland	1–0	–	1–2	3–0	6	3	0	3	8	5	6
Sweden	1–2	0–2	–	3–1	6	3	0	3	8	9	6
Norway	1–3	2–1	0–2	–	6	1	0	5	5	15	2

Group IV

	Spn.	Rum.	Sct.	Den.	P	W	D	L	F	A	Pts
SPAIN	–	1–1	1–1	2–0	6	3	3	0	10	6	9
Rumania	2–2	–	1–1	6–1	6	1	5	0	11	6	7
Scotland	1–2	1–1	–	3–1	6	2	3	1	8	6	7
Denmark	1–2	0–0	0–1	–	6	0	1	5	3	14	1

Group V

	Neth.	Pol.	It.	Fin.	P	W	D	L	F	A	Pts
NETHERLANDS	–	3–0	3–1	4–1	6	4	0	2	14	8	8
Poland	4–1	–	0–0	3–0	6	3	2	1	9	5	8
Italy	1–0	0–0	–	0–0	6	2	3	1	3	3	7
Finland	1–3	1–2	0–1	–	6	0	1	5	3	13	1

Group VI

	USSR	R.I.	Tur.	Swtz.	P	W	D	L	F	A	Pts
U.S.S.R.	–	2–1	3–0	4–1	6	4	0	2	10	6	8
Rep. of Ireland	3–0	–	4–0	2–1	6	3	1	2	11	5	7
Turkey	1–0	1–1	–	2–1	6	2	2	2	5	10	6
Switzerland	0–1	1–0	1–1	–	6	1	1	4	5	10	3

Group VII

	Bel.	E.G.	Fr.	Ice.	P	W	D	L	F	A	Pts
BELGIUM	–	1–2	2–1	1–0	6	3	2	1	6	3	8
East Germany	0–0	–	2–1	1–1	6	2	3	1	8	7	7
France	0–0	2–2	–	3–0	6	1	3	2	7	6	5
Iceland	0–2	2–1	0–0	–	6	1	2	3	3	8	4

Group VIII

	W.G.	Gr.	Bul.	Mal.							
WEST GERMANY.........	–	1–1	1–0	8–0	6	3	3	0	14	4	9
Greece....................	2–2	–	2–1	4–0	6	2	3	1	12	9	7
Bulgaria	1–1	3–3	–	5–0	6	2	2	2	12	7	6
Malta	0–1	2–0	0–2	–	6	1	0	5	2	20	2

Quarter-Finals

A	Netherlands	*v*	Belgium	B	Spain	*v*	W. Germany
	Belgium	*v*	Netherlands		W. Germany	*v*	Spain
C	Yugoslavia	*v*	Wales	D	Czechoslovakia	*v*	Soviet Union
	Wales	*v*	Yugoslavia		Soviet Union	*v*	Czechoslovakia

Semi-Finals

Winner of D *v* Winner of A
Winner of C *v* Winner of B

FINAL

NORTHERN IRELAND

A 16. 4. 75 Northern Ireland............1 Yugoslavia.................0 — Belfast (EFC)
        (Hamilton)
B 17. 5. 75 Northern Ireland............0 England...................0 — Belfast (BHC)
C 20. 5. 75 Scotland....................3 Northern Ireland............0 — Glasgow (BHC)
        (MacDougall, Dalglish,
        Parlane)
D 23. 5. 75 Northern Ireland............1 Wales.....................0 — Belfast (BHC)
        (Finney)
E 3. 9. 75 Northern Ireland............1 Sweden....................2 — Belfast (EFC)
        (Hunter)   (Sjoberg, Torstensson)
F 29. 10. 75 Northern Ireland............3 Norway....................0 — Belfast (EFC)
        (Morgan, McIlroy,
        Hamilton)
G 19. 11. 75 Yugoslavia.................1 Northern Ireland............0 — Belgrade (EFC)
        (Oblak)

	A	B	C	D	E	F	G
Jennings.........	G	G	G	G	G	G	G
Rice.............	RB	RB	RB	LB	RB	RB	RB
Nicholl.........	RCB	RCB	RCB	RCB	RCB	RCB	RCB
Hunter.........	LCB	LCB	LCB	LCB	LCB	LCB	LCB
Nelson..........	LB	—	—	—	LB	LB	—
O'Kane..........	—	LB	LB	—	—	—	LB
P. Scott.........	—	—	—	RB	—	—	—
Hamilton........	RH	RH¹	—	—	CF¹	RH	RH
Clements........	CH	CH	CH	CH	CH	—	CH
Jamison.........	—	—	—	—	—	CH	LH²
O'Neill.........	LH	LH	LH	—	—	—	—
Jackson.........	LF	LF	RH	LH	LH	LH	LH¹
Spence.........	RF	RF	RF	RF	RF	—	—
McIlroy........	CF	CF	CF	CF	LF	RF	RF
Morgan..........	—	—	—	—	CF²	CF	CF
Blair...........	—	—	—	RH	RH	—	—
Finney..........	—	RH²	LF	LF	—	LF	LF

ENGLAND

A 12. 3. 75 England .... 2 (Bell, Macdonald) West Germany .... 0 — Wembley
B 16. 4. 75 England .... 5 (Macdonald 5) Cyprus .... 0 — Wembley (EFC)
C 11. 5. 75 Cyprus .... 0 England .... 1 (Keegan) — Limassol (EFC)
D 17. 5. 75 Northern Ireland .... 0 England .... 0 — Belfast (BHC)
E 21. 5. 75 England .... 2 (Johnson 2) Wales .... 2 (Toshack, Griffiths) — Wembley (BHC)
F 24. 5. 75 England .... 5 (Francis 2, Beattie, Bell, Johnson) Scotland .... 1 (Rioch) — Wembley (BHC)
G 3. 9. 75 Switzerland .... 1 (Muller) England .... 2 (Keegan, Channon) — Basle
H 30. 10. 75 Czechoslovakia .... 2 (Nehoda, Galis) England .... 1 (Channon) — Bratislava (EFC)
I 19. 11. 75 Portugal .... 1 (Rodrigues) England .... 1 (Channon) — Lisbon (EFC)

	A	B	C	D	E	F	G	H	I
Clemence	G	—	G	G	G	G	G	G	G
Shilton	—	G	—	—	—	—	—	—	—
Whitworth	RB	—	RB	RB	RB	RB	RB	—	RB
Madeley	—	RB	—	—	—	—	—	RB	CH¹
Todd	RCB	RCB	RCB	RCB	RCB	RCB	RCB	RCB	RCB
Watson	LCB	LCB	LCB	LCB	LCB	LCB	LCB	LCB²	LCB
McFarland	—	—	—	—	—	—	—	LCB¹	—
Gillard	LB	—	—	—	LB	—	—	LB	—
Beattie	—	LB	LB¹	—	—	LB	LB	—	LB
Hughes	—	—	LB²	LB	—	—	—	—	—
Ball	RH	RH	RH	RH	RH	RH	—	—	—
G. Francis	—	—	—	—	CH	LH	RH	RH	RH
Bell	CH	CH	CH	CH	—	CH	CH	CH	—
Hudson	LH	LH	—	—	—	—	—	—	—
Keegan	LF	LF	LH	LF	—	LF¹	LF	LH	LF
Viljoen	—	—	—	LH	LH	—	—	—	—
Currie	—	—	—	—	—	—	LH	—	—
Brooking	—	—	—	—	—	—	—	—	LH
Channon	RF	RF¹	LF	CF²	RF¹	RF	RF	RF¹	RF
Thomas	—	RF²	RF¹	—	LF	LF²	—	RF²	CF²
Tueart	—	—	RF²	RF	—	—	—	—	—
Little	—	—	—	—	RF²	—	—	—	—
Macdonald	CF	CF	CF	CF¹	—	—	CF²	CF	CF¹
Johnson	—	—	—	—	CF	CF	CF¹	—	—
Clarke	—	—	—	—	—	—	—	LF	CH²

CZECHOSLOVAKIA

A	31. 3. 75	Czechoslovakia............1 (Nehoda)	Rumania...................1 (Kun)	—	Prague
B	20. 4. 75	Czechoslovakia............4 (Panenka 3, Masny)	Cyprus 0	—	Prague (EFC)
C	30. 4. 75	Czechoslovakia............5 (Bicovsky 2, Nehoda 2, Petras)	Portugal 0	—	Prague (EFC)
D	7. 6. 75	Austria 0	Czechoslovakia............0	—	Vienna
E	24. 9. 75	Czechoslovakia............1 (Masny)	Switzerland ....1 (Risi)	—	Brno
F	15. 10. 75	Czechoslovakia............1 (Nehoda)	Hungary ....1 (Varadi)	—	Bratislava
G	30. 10. 75	Czechoslovakia............2 (Nehoda, Galis)	England ....1 (Channon)	—	Bratislava (EFC)
H	12. 11. 75	Portugal ....1 (Nene)	Czechoslovakia............1 (Ondrus)	—	Porto (EFC)
I	19. 11. 75	Czechoslovakia............1 (Bicovsky)	East Germany ....1 (Weise)	—	Brno (OQ)
J	23. 11. 75	Cyprus 0	Czechoslovakia............3 (Nehoda, Bicovsky, Masny)	—	Limassol (EFC)

	A	B	C	D	E	F	G	H	I	J
Viktor	G	G	G	G	G	G	G	G	G	G
Pivarnik	RB	RB	RB	RB	RB	—	RB	RB	RB	RB
Dobias	—	—	—	LCB	LB²	RB	LB²	RF²	—	—
Ondrus	RCB	RCB	RCB	RCB¹	LCB	RCB	LCB	LCB	LCB	RCB
Jos. Capkovic	LCB	LCB¹	LCB	—	RCB	—	—	—	—	—
Jurkemik	—	—	—	RCB²	—	LCB¹	RCB	RCB	RCB	LCB
Dvorak	—	—	—	—	—	LCB²	—	—	—	—
Koubek	LB	LB	LB¹	—	LB¹	—	—	—	—	—
Rygel	—	—	—	LB	—	—	—	—	—	—
K. Gogh	—	—	—	—	—	LB	LB¹	LB	LB	LB
Bicovsky	RH	RH	RH	RH	RH	RH	CH	RH	RH	RH
Panenka	CH	CH	—	—	LH²	—	—	—	—	—
Knapp	—	—	CH¹	CH	CH	—	LH	—	—	—
Medvid	—	—	CH²	—	—	—	—	—	—	CH²
Pollak	—	—	—	—	—	CH	RH	CH	CH	CH¹
Svoboda	—	—	LB²	—	—	—	—	—	—	—
Gajdusek	LH¹	LH	LH	LH	LH¹	—	—	—	—	—
Moder	—	—	—	—	—	LH	—	LH	LH	LH
Masny	RF	RF	RF	—	RF¹	RF	RF	RF¹	RF	RF
Svehlik	CF¹	CF	—	RF	—	—	—	—	—	CF¹
Jurkanin	CF²	—	—	—	—	—	—	—	—	—
Petras	—	LCB²	CF	CF¹	RF²	—	—	—	—	—
Stratil	LH²	—	—	CF²	—	—	—	—	—	—
Kroupa	—	—	—	—	—	—	—	—	CF²	—
Galis	—	—	—	—	LF	CF¹	CF	CF¹	CF¹	—
F. Vesely	—	—	—	—	—	CF²	—	CF²	—	CF²
Nehoda	LF	LF	LF	—	CF	LF	LF	LF	LF	LF
Jarkovsky	—	—	—	LF	—	—	—	—	—	—

WALES

A 16. 4. 75 Hungary ....1 Wales ....2 — Budapest (EFC)
 (Branikovits) (Toshack, Mahoney)

B 1. 5. 75 Luxembourg...............1 Wales ....3 — Luxembourg (EFC)
 (Phillip) (Reece, James 2)

C 17. 5. 75 Wales ....2 Scotland ....2 — Cardiff (BHC)
 (Toshack, Flynn) (Jackson, Rioch)

D 21. 5. 75 England ....2 Wales ....2 — Wembley (BHC)
 (Johnson 2) (Toshack, Griffiths)

E 23. 5. 75 Northern Ireland ....1 Wales ....0 — Belfast (BHC)
 (Finney)

F 19. 11. 75 Wales ....1 Austria ....0 — Wrexham (EFC)
 (Griffiths)

	A	B	C	D	E	F		A	B	C	D	E	F
D. Davies	G	G	G	G	G	—	Yorath	RH	RH	RH	—	—	RF
Lloyd	—	—	—	—	—	G	Mahoney	CH	CH	CH	CH	CH	CH
Thomas	RB	RB	RB	RB	RB	RB	Griffiths	LH	LH[1]	—	RH	RH	RH
J. Roberts	RCB	—	RCB	RCB	—	—	Flynn	LF[2]	LH[2]	LH	LH	LH	LH
D. Roberts	—	RCB	—	—	RCB	—	Reece	RF[1]	RF	RF	—	RF	—
Phillips	LCB	LCB	LCB	LCB	LCB	LCB	Smallman	RF[2]	—	—	RF[1]	—	CF
Evans	—	—	—	—	—	RCB	Showers	—	—	—	RF[2]	CF	—
Page	LB	LB	LB	LB	LB	—	Toshack	CF	CF	CF	CF	—	—
Joey Jones	—	—	—	—	—	LB	James	LF[1]	LF	LF	LF	LF	LF

YUGOSLAVIA

A 16. 4. 75 Northern Ireland ....1 Yugoslavia ....0 — Belfast (EFC)
 (Hamilton)

B 31. 5. 75 Yugoslavia ....3 Netherlands ....0 — Belgrade
 (Savic, Popivoda, Ivejic)

C 4. 6. 75 Sweden ....1 Yugoslavia ....2 — Stockholm (EFC)
 (Edstrom) (Katalinski, Ivejic)

D 9. 6. 75 Norway....................1 Yugoslavia ....3 — Oslo (EFC)
 (Thunberg) (Buljan, Bogicevic, Savic)

E 15. 10. 75 Yugoslavia ....3 Sweden ....0 — Zagreb (EFC)
 (Oblak, Vladic, Vabec)

F 19. 11. 75 Yugoslavia ....1 Northern Ireland ....0 — Belgrade (EFC)
 (Oblak)

	A	B	C*	D	E	F		A	B	C*	D	E	F
O. Petrovic	G	G	G	G	G	G	Vladic	RF[2]	LH[1]	OR	LH	LH	LH
Buljan	RB	RB	RB	RB	RB	RB	Ivejic	—	LH[2]	LCF[2]	—	—	—
Katalinski	RCB	RCB[1]	LCB	RCB	RCB	RCB	Vukotic	RF[1]	—	—	—	—	RF
Novoslovic	—	RCB[2]	—	—	—	—	Popivoda	—	RF	RCF	RF	—	—
Peruzovic	LCB	—	—	—	—	—	Vabec	—	—	—	—	RF	—
Bogicevic	—	LCB	RH	RH	—	—	Milkovic	CF[2]	—	—	—	—	—
Muzinic	RH	RH	RCB	LCB	LCB	LCB	Savic	—	CF	LCF[1]	CF	—	—
Jerkovic	CF[1]	—	—	—	RH	RH	Surjak	LF	LF[1]	OL	LF	CF	CF
Oblak	CH	CH	LH	CH	CH	CH	Dzajic	—	—	—	—	LF	LF
Jankovic	LH	—	—	—	—	—	V. Petrovic	—	LF[2]	—	—	—	—
Hadziabdic	LB	LB	LB	LB	LB	LB							

*4-2-4

SCOTLAND

A	5. 2. 75	Spain .... 1 (Megido)	Scotland 1	— Valencia (EFC) (Jordan)
B	16. 4. 75	Sweden .... 1 (Sjoberg)	Scotland 1	— Gothenburg (MacDougall)
C	13. 5. 75	Scotland .... 1 (Artur o.g.)	Portugal 0	— Glasgow
D	17. 5. 75	Wales .... 2 (Toshack, Flynn)	Scotland 2	— Cardiff (BHC) (Jackson, Rioch)
E	20. 5. 75	Scotland .... 3 (MacDougall, Dalglish, Parlane)	Northern Ireland 0	— Glasgow (BHC)
F	24. 5. 75	England .... 5 (Francis 2, Beattie, Bell, Johnson)	Scotland .... 1 (Rioch)	— Wembley (BHC)
G	1. 6. 75	Rumania.................. 1 (Georgescu)	Scotland .... 1 (McQueen)	— Bucharest (EFC)
H	3. 9. 75	Denmark.................. 0	Scotland .... 1 (Harper)	— Copenhagen (EFC)
I	29. 10. 75	Scotland .... 3 (Dalglish, Rioch, MacDougall)	Denmark .... 1 (Bastrup)	— Glasgow (EFC)
J	17. 12. 75	Scotland .... 1 (Rioch)	Rumania.................. 1 (Crisan)	— Glasgow (EFC)

	A	B	C	D	E	F	G	H	I	J
Harvey	G	—	—	—	—	—	—	G	G	—
Kennedy	—	G	G	G	G	G	—	—	—	—
Jim Brown	—	—	—	—	—	—	G	—	—	—
Cruickshank	—	—	—	—	—	—	—	—	—	G
Jardine	RB	RB	RB	RB	RB	RB	—	—	—	—
Brownlie	—	—	—	—	—	—	—	—	—	RB
McQueen	RCB	—	LCB	LCB	LCB	LCB	LCB	LCB	—	—
Munro	—	RCB	—	RCB²	RCB	RCB	RCB	—	—	—
Buchan	LCB	—	RCB	—	—	—	—	RCB	—	—
Jackson	—	LCB	—	RCB¹	—	—	—	—	RCB	LCB
Greig	—	—	—	—	—	—	—	—	LCB	—
McGrain	LB	LB	LB	LB	LB	LB	RB	RB	RB	—
A. Forsyth	—	—	—	—	—	—	LB	LB	—	—
Houston	—	—	—	—	—	—	—	—	LB	—
Donachie	—	—	—	—	—	—	—	—	—	LB
Bremner	RH	—	—	—	—	—	—	RH	—	—
Robinson	—	RH¹	—	—	LH¹	—	RH²	—	—	—
Rioch	—	—	RH¹	RH	RH	RH	RH¹	LH	RH	RH
Macari	—	LF¹	RH²	LH	—	CF²	CF¹	—	—	—
Dalglish	CH	CH	LH	CH	CH	CH	CH	CH	LF	LF¹
Hartford	—	—	—	—	—	—	—	—	CH	CH
Burns	LH¹	—	—	—	—	—	—	—	—	—
Souness	—	LH	—	—	—	—	—	—	—	—
Conn	—	—	—	—	LH²	LH	—	—	—	—
Miller	—	—	—	—	—	—	LH	—	—	—
Gemmill	—	—	—	—	—	—	—	—	LH	LH
Cooke	RF	—	CH¹	—	—	—	—	—	—	—
Parlane	CF²	RF	RF	RF	RF	RF	RF	—	CF²	—
Lorimer	—	—	—	—	—	—	—	RF	RF	RF²
Doyle	—	—	—	—	—	—	—	—	—	RF¹
Jordan	CF¹	—	—	—	—	—	—	—	—	—
MacDougall	—	CF	CF	CF	CF	CF¹	—	—	CF¹	LF²
Harper	—	—	—	—	—	—	—	CF	—	—
A. Gray	—	—	—	—	—	—	—	—	—	CF
Hutchinson	LF	—	LF	—	—	LF²	CF²	LF¹	—	—
A. Duncan	—	RH²	CH²	LF	LF	LF¹	LF	LF²	—	—
Wilson	LH²	—	—	—	—	—	—	—	—	—
D. Johnstone	—	LF²	—	—	—	—	—	—	—	—

RUMANIA

A	19. 3. 75	Turkey ....1 (Cemil)	Rumania................1 (Lucescu)	—	Istanbul	
B	31. 3. 75	Czechoslovakia.............1 (Nehoda)	Rumania................1 (Kun)	—	Prague	
C	17. 4. 75	Spain.....................1 (Velasquez)	Rumania................1 (Crisan)	—	Madrid (EFC)	
D	10. 5. 75	Rumania..................6 (Georgescu 2, Crisan 2, Lucescu, Dinu)	Denmark................1 (Dahl)	—	Bucharest (EFC)	
E	1. 6. 75	Rumania................1 (Georgescu)	Scotland ....1 (McQueen)	—	Bucharest (EFC)	
F	24. 9. 75	Greece...................1 (Sarafis)	Rumania................1 (Dumitru)	—	Salonika	
G	12. 10. 75	Rumania................2 (Iordanescu, Dinu)	Turkey ....2 (Gökmen, Cemil)	—	Bucharest	
H	16. 11. 75	Rumania................2 (Georgescu, Iordanescu)	Spain................2 (Villar, Santillana)	—	Bucharest (EFC)	
I	29. 11. 75	Rumania................2 (Troi, Hajnal)	U.S.S.R................2 (Kolotov, Konkov)	—	Bucharest	
J	17. 12. 75	Scotland ....1 (Rioch)	Rumania................1 (Crisan)	—	Glasgow (EFC)	

	A	B	C	D	E	F	G	H	I	J
Raducanu	G	G	G	G	G	—	G²	G	G¹	G
Moraru	—	—	—	—	—	G	G¹	—	G²	—
Cheran	RB	RB	RB	RB	RB	RB	—	—	—	RB
Matescu	—	—	—	—	—	—	—	—	RB	—
G. Sandu	RCB	LCB	RCB	RCB	LCB	LCB	RCB	RCB	RCB	RCB
Satmareanu	—	RCB	LCB	LCB	RCB	RCB	LCB	LCB	—	LCB
Sames	LCB	—	—	—	—	—	—	—	LCB	—
Anghelini	LB	LB	LB	LB	LB	LB	RB	RB	—	LB
Hajnal	—	—	—	—	—	—	LB	—	LF²	—
Lucuta	—	—	—	—	—	—	—	LB	LB	—
Dumitru	RH	CH	LH	RH¹	RH	RH	RH	—	—	—
Romila	—	—	—	—	—	—	—	—	—	RH
Dinu	CH	RH	—	CH	LH	CH	CH	LH	CH	CH
Balaci	—	—	RH	RH²	CH²	—	LH²	—	RH¹	—
Georgescu	LH²	LH	CH	LH	CH¹	—	CF	RH	LH	CF
Dobrin	—	—	—	CF¹	CF¹	—	LH¹	CH	RH²	—
Troi	RF²	—	—	—	—	—	—	—	CF	—
Nunweiler	—	RF	RF¹	—	—	—	—	—	—	—
Crisan	RF¹	—	RF²	RF	RF	—	RF²	CF²	—	RF²
Fazekas	—	—	—	—	—	RF	RF¹	—	—	—
Boloni	—	—	—	—	—	LH	—	—	—	LH
M. Sandu	—	—	—	—	—	—	—	RF¹	—	—
Kun	CF	CF	CF¹	CF²	CF²	—	—	—	—	—
Iordanescu	LH¹	—	CF²	—	—	CF	LF	RF²	RF	LF
Zamfir	—	—	—	—	—	—	CF¹	—	—	—
Lucescu	LF	LF	LF	LF	LF	LF	—	LF	LF¹	RF¹

GREECE

A 23. 3. 75 Malta .... 2 Greece .... 0 — Valetta (EFC)
    (Aquilina, Magro)

B 2. 4. 75 Cyprus .... 1 Greece .... 2 — Nicosia
    (Tasso)   (Anastasiadis, Kritikopoulos)

C 4. 6. 75 Greece .... 4 Malta .... 0 — Salonika (EFC)
    (Mavros, Antoniadis, Papaioannou, Iosifidis)

D 24. 9. 75 Greece .... 1 Rumania .... 1 — Salonika
    (Sarafis)   (Dumitru)

E 12. 10. 75 West Germany .... 1 Greece .... 1 — Dusseldorf (EFC)
    (Heynckes)   (Delikaris)

F 30. 12. 75 Italy .... 3 Greece .... 2 — Florence
    (Pulici 2, Savoldi)   (Kritikopoulos, Sarafis)

	A	B	C	D	E	F
Konstantinou	G	—	—	G	—	—
Sidiropoulos	—	G	—	—	—	—
Papastratos	—	—	G	—	—	—
Kelesidis	—	—	—	—	G	G
Pallas	RB	RB	RB	RB	LCB	RB
Kyrastas	—	—	—	LF²	RB	RCB
Iosifidis	RCB	RCB	LCB	LCB	—	—
Pellios	—	LCB	RCB¹	—	—	—
Apostolidis	—	—	RH	RCB	RCB²	—
Synetopoulos	—	—	—	—	RCB¹	LCB
Siokos	LCB	—	—	—	—	—
Foiros	LB	—	LB	LB	LB	LB
Nikolaou	CH	LB	RCB²	CF²	—	LF³
Dimitriou	RH¹	—	—	—	—	—
Paridis	RH²	LF	—	—	—	—
Tsamis	—	RH	—	—	—	—

	A	B	C	D	E	F
Koudas	—	—	—	RH	LH¹	LH
Terzanidis	—	LH	—	—	RH	CH
Sarafis	RF	—	—	LH	CH	RH
Anastasiadis	—	CH	RF	—	—	—
Papaioannou	LH¹	—	CH	CH	RF	CF
Domazos	LH²	—	—	—	—	—
Mavros	—	—	LH	—	—	—
Kritikopoulos	LF	RF	—	CF¹	CF	RF
Aslanidis	—	—	LF	RF	LH²	—
Antoniadis	CF	—	CF¹	—	—	—
Elefterakis	—	CF	—	—	—	—
Kalambakas	—	—	CF²	—	—	—
Ardiziglou	—	—	—	LF¹	—	—
Delikaris	—	—	—	—	LF	LF²
Karavitis	—	—	—	—	—	LF¹

SPAIN

A 5. 2. 75 Spain .... 1 Scotland .... 1 — Valencia (EFC)
    (Megido)   (Jordan)

B 17. 4. 75 Spain .... 1 Rumania .... 1 — Madrid (EFC)
    (Velasquez)   (Crisan)

C 12. 10. 75 Spain .... 2 Denmark .... 0 — Barcelona (EFC)
    (Pirri, Capon)

D 16. 11. 75 Rumania .... 2 Spain .... 2 — Bucharest (EFC)
    (Georgescu, Iordanescu)   (Villar, Santillana)

	A	B	C	D
Iribar	G	G	—	—
Miguel Angel	—	—	G	G
Sol	RB	—	—	RB
Ramos	—	—	RB	—
Benito	RCB	RCB	RCB	RCB
Camacho	LCB	RB	—	LB
Pirri	—	LCB	RH	LCB
Migueli	—	—	LCB	CH
Costas	LB	—	—	—
Capon	—	LB	LB	—
Claramunt	RH	—	—	—
Del Bosque	—	RH	CH¹	LH
Villar	CH	—	—	RH

	A	B	C	D
Rojo	—	LH	—	LF¹
Quini	RF	—	—	RF¹
Velasquez	—	CH¹	—	—
Irureta	—	CH²	—	—
Garate	CF¹	RF	—	—
Megido	CF²	—	—	—
Marcial	—	—	RF	—
Satrustequie	—	—	—	RF²
Asensi	LH	—	CH²	—
Santillana	—	CF	LH	CF
Solsona	—	—	CF	—
Rexach	LF	LF	LF	—
Fortes	—	—	—	LF²

SOVIET UNION (U.S.S.R.)

A 2. 4. 75 U.S.S.R. .3 Turkey .0 — Kiev (EFC)
(Kolotov 2, Blochin)

B 18. 5. 75 U.S.S.R. . . . . .2 Rep. of Ireland . . . . .1 — Kiev (EFC)
(Kolotov, Blochin) (Hand)

C 8. 6. 75 U.S.S.R. . . . . .1 Italy .0 — Moscow
(Konkov)

D 12. 10. 75 Switzerland . . . . .0 U.S.S.R. . . . . .1 — Zurich (EFC)
(Muntian)

E 12. 11. 75 U.S.S.R. . . . . .4 Switzerland . . . . .1 — Kiev (EFC)
(Onischenko 2, Konkov, (Risi)
Veremejev)

F 23. 11. 75 Turkey .1 U.S.S.R. . . . . .0 — Izmir (EFC)
(Reschko o.g.)

G 29. 11. 75 Rumania . . . . .2 U.S.S.R. . . . . .2 — Bucharest
(Troi, Hajnal) (Kolotov, Konkov)

	A	B	C*	D	E	F*	G
Rudakov	G	G	G	G	G	G	—
Astapovski	—	—	—	—	—	—	G
Konkov	RB[1]	LB	RH	RH	RH[1]	RB	RH
Burjak	RB[2]	RF	LB	LH[1]	CF	RH[2]	CF
Trochkin	RH	RB	RB	RB	RB	—	RB
Matvijenko	RCB	RCB	LCB	—	—	—	—
Fomenko	LCB	LCB	RCB	RCB[1]	RCB	LCB	RCB
Reschko	LB	RH[2]	LCH[2]	RCB[2]	—	LCH	LB
Zujev	—	—	—	—	—	RCB	—
Zviaguintzev	—	—	—	LCB	LCB	LB	LCB
Lovtchev	—	—	—	LB	LB	—	—
Muntian	CH	RH[1]	RCH	CH	CH[1]	RH[1]	—
Sacharov	—	—	—	LH[2]	RH[2]	—	—
Veremejev	CF	CH[1]	LCH[1]	CF	LH	RCH	CH
Kolotov	LH	LH	LH	—	CH[2]	LH	LH
Onischenko	RF[1]	CF	RF	RF	RF	RF	RF
Federov	RF[2]	CH[2]	—	—	—	—	—
Blochin	LF	LF	LF	LF	LF	LF	LF[1]
Andriassian	—	—	—	—	—	—	LF[2]

*4–4–2

BELGIUM

A 30. 4. 75 Belgium .1 Netherlands . . . . .0 — Antwerp
(Lambert)

B 6. 9. 75 Belgium .1 Iceland .0 — Brussels (EFC)
(Lambert)

C 29. 9. 75 Belgium .1 East Germany . . . . .2 — Brussels (EFC)
(Puis) (Ducke, Hafner)

D 16. 11. 75 France .0 Belgium .0 — Paris (EFC)

	A	B	C	D*			A	B	C	D*
Piot	G	G	G	G	Polleunis	—	LH	RH[1]	—
Van Binst	RB	RB	—	RB	Jensens	—	—	RH[2]	—
Gerets	—	—	RB	—	Coeck	CH	—	LH	LH
Dewalque	RCB	LCB	LCB	—	Verheyen	—	CH	—	RCH
Broos	—	RCB	—	—	Van der Eycken . . .	—	—	—	LCH
Van den Daele	LCB	—	RCB	LCB	Coot	LH	—	—	—
Leekens	—	—	—	RCB	Van der Elst	RF	—	—	—
Caers	LB[1]	—	—	—	Lambert	CF	RF	—	LF[1]
Dockx	LB[2]	—	—	LB	Devrindt	—	CF	RF	—
Martens	—	LB	LB	—	Van Gool	—	—	—	RF
Van Moer	RH	—	—	—	Teugels	LF	LF	CF	LF[2]
Cools	—	RH	CH	RH	Puis	—	—	LF	—

*4–4–2

NETHERLANDS

A 30. 4. 75 Belgium.....................1 Netherlands ....0 — Antwerp
      (Lambert)

B 17. 5. 75 West Germany..............1 Netherlands ....1 — Frankfurt
      (Wimmer) (Van Hanegem)

C 31. 5. 75 Yugoslavia ....3 Netherlands ....0 — Belgrade
      (Savic, Popivoda, Ivejic)

D   3. 9. 75 Netherlands ....4 Finland ....1 — Nijmegen (EFC)
      (Van der Kuylen 3, Lubse) (Patelainen)

E 10. 9. 75 Poland......................4 Netherlands ....1 — Chorzow (EFC)
      (Szarmach 2, Lato, Gadocha) (R. Van der Kerkhof)

F 15. 10. 75 Netherlands ....3 Poland......................0 — Amsterdam (EFC)
      (Neeskens, Geels, Thijssen)

G 22. 11. 75 Italy ....1 Netherlands ....0 — Rome (EFC)
      (Capello)

	A	B	C	D	E	F	G
Schrijvers	G	G	—	—	—	G	G
Jongbloed	—	—	G	—	—	—	—
Van Beveren	—	—	—	G	G	—	—
Suurbier	RB	RB	—	RB	RB	RB	RB
Van Rijnsoever	—	—	RB	—	—	—	—
Rijsbergen	RCB	RCB	LCB	—	—	—	—
Overweg	—	RH²	RCB	LCB	LCB	—	—
Van Kray	LCB	LCB	—	RCB	RCB	RCB	LCB
Krijgh	—	—	—	—	—	LCB	RCB
Krol	LB	LB	—	LB	LB	LB	LB
Everse	RH²	—	LB	—	—	—	—
Thijssen	RH¹	RH¹	—	—	—	LH	LH
Neeskens	—	—	RH	—	CH	CH	—
Peters	CH	CH	CH	RH	—	—	RH
Jansen	—	—	LF²	CH	RH	RH	CH
Van Hanegem	LH¹	LH	—	LH	LH¹	—	—
Arntz	LH²	—	CF¹	—	—	—	—
Vosmaer	—	—	LH	—	—	—	—
Geels	—	—	—	—	LH²	RF	CF
Kist	RF	LF²	RF	—	—	—	—
R. Van der Kerkhof	—	RF	—	RF	RF	LF	RF
Zuidema	CF	LF¹	—	—	—	—	—
Van der Kuylen	—	CF	—	LF	LF	—	—
Otto	—	—	CF²	—	—	—	—
Lubse	—	—	—	CF	—	—	—
Cruyff	—	—	—	—	CF	CF	—
Rensenbrink	LF	—	—	—	—	—	—
Van Marwijk	—	—	LF¹	—	—	—	—
W. Van der Kerkhof	—	—	—	—	—	—	LF¹
Notten	—	—	—	—	—	—	LF²

WEST GERMANY

A 12. 3. 75   England 2   West Germany .... 0 — Wembley
           (Bell, Macdonald)

B 27. 4. 75   Bulgaria 1   West Germany .... 1 — Sofia (EFC)
           (Kolev)   (Ritschel)

C 17. 5. 75   West Germany 1   Netherlands .... 1 — Frankfurt
           (Wimmer)   (Van Hanegem)

D 3. 9. 75   Austria 0   West Germany .... 2 — Vienna
           (Beer 2)

E 11. 10. 75   West Germany 1   Greece..................... 1 — Dusseldorf (EFC)
           (Heynckes)   (Delikaris)

F 19. 11. 75   West Germany 1   Bulgaria .... 0 — Stuttgart (EFC)
           (Heynckes)

G 20. 12. 75   Turkey 0   West Germany .... 5 — Istanbul
           (Heynckes 2, Worm 2, Beer)

	A	B	C	D	E	F	G
Maier	G	G	G	G	G	G	—
Kargus	—	—	—	—	—	—	G
Vogts	RB	RB	RB	LB	LB	RB	RB
Kaltz	—	—	—	RB	RB	—	—
Beckenbauer	RCB	LCB	LCB	RCB¹	LCB	RCB	RCB
Schwarzenbeck	—	RCB	—	LCB¹	—	LCB	LCB
Kliemann	—	—	RCB	—	—	—	—
Korbel	LCB	CH²	CH	RH	RCB	—	LH
Danner	—	—	—	LCB²	—	CH	LH
Cullmann	RH	—	RH²	—	—	—	—
Netzer	—	RH	—	—	CH	—	—
Wimmer	LH¹	—	RH¹	CH¹	—	RH	CH¹
Beer	—	—	LH	RCB²	RH	CF	CF
Bonhof	LB	LH	LB	—	—	—	CH²
Breitner	—	LB	—	—	LH	—	—
Dietz	—	—	—	—	—	LB	LB¹
Reichel	—	—	—	—	—	—	LB²
Worm	—	—	—	—	—	—	RH²
Stielike	—	—	—	LH	—	LH	RH¹
Flohe	CH	—	—	—	—	—	—
Hoeness	—	CH¹	—	—	—	—	—
Keller	—	—	—	CH²	—	—	—
H. Kremers	LH²	—	—	—	—	—	—
Ritschel	RF	RF	RF	—	—	—	—
Seel	—	CF	CF	RF	—	—	—
Holzenbein	LF	LF²	LF	LF	RF	RF	RF
Kostedde	CF¹	—	—	—	CF	—	—
Heynckes	CF²	LF¹	—	—	LF	LF	LF
Gersdorff	—	—	—	CF	—	—	—